By the Grace of God, the Skin of My Teeth... and Friends

Betty Ferguson

PublishAmerica
Baltimore

First printing

ISBN: 1-4241-8333-2
PUBLISHED BY PUBLISHAMERICA, LLLP
www.publishamerica.com
Baltimore

Printed in the United States of America

*Many people make a huge difference in our lives.
Some are with us still and some are not.
My first published book is dedicated to all the angels in my life.*

My son, TJ (1974-1996), my husband, Jim (1941-1998) and my Dad, Ken (1925-2005).

And to those angels who helped me hang on through the thin times: My son, Jason, my mom, Alice, and my sister, Althea. My friends, Sheila Barker, Grace Jones, Bernie Rhodes, Heather Kniffen, Gary Baute, Betsy Bangert, Kathy Buen, Doug McFarlin, Nick and Priscilla Buis, J.R Honeycut, Brian Wies, Lillian Butler, Gloria Bahn, and Bill Berry.

I have also had the love and support of so many other family members and friends, and consider them a blessing each and every day. They say that it takes a village to raise a child…with me it takes a universe to make my world complete.

Introduction—It's like this...

It is thought that when one writes a book, they are "an expert" in the field they are writing about. I am certainly no expert in anything, but when it comes to the subjects in this book, I can definitely say, "been there, done that"...and survived, and thrived!

While there are many things I have not experienced in my fifty-seven years, most of them are horrific events that do not occur to everyone. When it comes to the day-to-day living, struggles and triumphs of life, I've got most of that covered.

I have been unbelievably happy, as sad as you can get, and angry as can be. I have been judgmental and judged, and I have received and given unconditional love and forgiveness.

I have lived a comfortable life, been a millionaire, been *poorer* than a church mouse, declared bankruptcy, and been evicted and homeless, and bounced back from adversity each time.

I have paid hundreds of thousands of dollars for a house, offshore powerboat, and five Harleys *in cash*, and literally not had a dollar to my name, and I have gotten my utilities shut off more times than I can count.

I have had the joy of being a mom of two boys, and the total devastation of the unexpected death of my oldest son, T.J. when he was twenty-two.

I have been SO angry with God, and SO impressed with how He just continued to love me and bless me anyway, as I got over it.

At twenty-one I married the man of my dreams, and ten years later had a horrendous two and one half year divorce.

Seven years later I married the love of my life, and he passed away eight years ago after thirteen wonderful years of marriage.

So, in my adult life, I have been single, married, divorced, single, married, widowed and single. Being "a single woman" at different ages is enough for a book unto itself!

I have had to beg for and borrow money both personally and professionally, which is a very humbling experience. I have also been on the giving end, without any thought of repayment.

I have been an employee, employer, and a self-employed entrepreneur, both unsuccessfully and successfully.

I have gone from wondering how to change my life to *knowing* what it takes...and *making it happen*! That is the journey I will share with you.

I firmly believe that God never gives you more than you can handle and then He gives you the strength to handle it. I have sometimes wondered why *my* plate always has to be so full, but I also know that God has a plan for me, and while the journey I have taken in these fifty-seven years has been a little rough at times, it has not hurt me at all. It has been a learning experience, one which has proven time and time again that the main ingredient to success in anything in life is FAITH. I have succeeded, and you can too.

Let me share my journey and what I have learned....

This Is How I See It...

It never ceases to amaze me that when life is good and things are going well, most people are so blasé about it and take it for granted. Even if you are extremely faith oriented…faith in God that is, you have to admit that when the bills are paid, the vehicles run fine, no major issue in your life is threatening your current "happy" existence, then you just let the days fly by, one after the other, without truly recognizing each and every miracle it takes to make that "happy" existence possible.

Those who attend church regularly might believe their good fortune is because they do live a faith-based life, saying their prayers daily, doing what they feel they can for others…and by living "the good life." The *good stuff* of house, transportation, plenty of clothes, food, toys and ability to buy an abundance of things they don't really *need*, but do want, comes from working hard and doing well in their chosen field. Or maybe just hanging onto a job for years, whether they enjoy it or not, to have a steady income that pays the bills. It is about their effort, what they have been able to accomplish, and their successes.

Does that mean that they don't ever have trials and tribulations, illness and death, financial difficulties, cars that break down or employment and kid issues? Definitely not. But they do have the faith it takes to look at those issues in a different light. Not as the end of the world, but as a bump in their road. Or sometimes a small mountain to climb! But they know they are not climbing it alone.

So…does that mean that those who don't go to church regularly or are not focused on a "faith based life" are doomed to a horrible life? Definitely not. Many "wealthy and successful" people do not go to church regularly. Some went to church when they were young, but do not go today. Some never give God a thought unless it is to blame him for things gone wrong. But their life seems to be going well.

If you are alive and going forward day by day, it is definitely by the Grace of God. All your body parts function 24/7 without your thought or input. Days turn into nights and back again without your help. There is no assistance needed from you for the seasons to change every year. You get the point. The days, months and years march on. And whether you attend church or not, the majority of people are just hanging out…and hanging on.

Life should be so much more than just hanging out and hanging on. We all have the opportunity each day to make a difference (for the better) in the lives of those we love, of those we don't even know, and in our own lives.

Most students go to school, come home and have homework to do, possibly a job or practice for a sport, and try to eek out a social life or spend their free time on the phone, computer IMing friends, or in front of TV/video games. Many adults split their day between work, family, housework, possibly some civic or church work and try desperately for a little time for themselves. Most single adults I know (no kids at home) spend their allotted time at work, and spend the rest of their time trying to find where the best entertainment for tonight is, then hanging out with their friends or trying to make new ones.

When was the last time that you:

-Stopped what you were doing to call someone who you don't talk to on a regular basis...just to say hi and let them know you were thinking of them?

-Took the time to call or visit with someone you know does not have a lot of family in the area?

-Talked to someone you see regularly, or a stranger, who does not appear to have a ton of friends and seems to feel less than adequate in the world? Hint: They are usually sitting alone and with their head down, but watching others around them. Just smiling and saying hi as you pass by is recognition they didn't have.

-Given someone who obviously does not have a dime some money, no matter what you think they might do with it, just because you are so blessed and you can? Not necessarily a lot, just some.

-Took the time to introduce yourself to a neighbor you never met (usually after years of living near them)?

Yesterday I was in the grocery store and there was a flyer on the floor in the checkout line. The lady two people in front of me stepped on it, got it off her shoe and moved forward in line. The guy in front of me picked it up and put it in the newspaper rack. If he hadn't, I would have. What would possess someone not to even bother to pick up a flyer that is going to be in everyone else's way? The line was stalled...we weren't that busy. Kudos to the guy in front of me.

On the other hand, earlier the same day my girlfriend and I were walking around a local festival when a lady with a baby carriage got a long messy piece of yellow tape stuck to her foot and could not get it off. We, and two other people walking by, walked right over to help her immediately. Again…we weren't that busy.

There are a multitude of opportunities in your day to positively affect the lives of others if you just look for them. You never know when a smile, a call, sending a short e-mail that is NOT a joke, or giving a helping hand makes an enormous difference in someone's day, or possibly entire week. When someone is looking at you, smile if nothing else. Don't just turn your head and act like you didn't see them. There's always time for at least a smile…after all, you always have them with you. And you aren't so busy you can't find one.

I am pretty sure that there is at least one instance in your every day where the phrase, "There, but for the Grace of God, go I" would apply. There is someone you see, know, think of, or hear about that would bring that phrase to mind.

My favorite phrase of that nature is a little different. "Here, *by* the Grace of God, go I" He makes it happen, ladies and gentlemen. The world doesn't go around all by itself…it goes around by the Grace of God.

Faith and Trust Go Hand in Hand

I paid my electric bill yesterday. Well, not all of it, but I had the minimum so they wouldn't shut of my electricity today. I have $12.50 in my checking account, $5.34 in my savings and probably $3.00 in my wallet...that's it, folks! My house phone/ DSL has been off for a couple of months, but I have a cell phone and got a wireless PC card by the grace of God and with the help of a great friend, Doug (one of my angels). I owe three months rent as of today—soon to be four, but God also gave me Brian, my wonderful landlord and friend (another angel) who is not a happy camper, but works with me on it because he knows in the end I will come up with the rent. I thank God, literally, for my angels every day. I scraped together enough for the water bill last month so that is okay for now, but I just got an e-mail that said my e-mail account has been shut off...again. On and on, round and round it has gone for the past few years. Sometimes up, sometimes down, but it always goes.

The ironic thing is that I know in my heart that soon it is more likely than not that I will again be VERY wealthy, and these issues will *never* be a concern to me again. I'll bet you think that I think I am going to win a huge lottery? Maybe (I am now in the right vibration for that), and I do still buy tickets (just in case— you can't win if you don't play). I used to ask God, on lottery days twice a week for years, to let me win because I would do *so much* good with that money. But that is not what I am focusing on now. I am focusing on receiving large sums of money on a regular basis. When exactly they arrive and how is not up to me. My job is to be open to possibilities and ready for the responsibility that will also arrive.

I have come to the realization that every time I ask God to make me wealthy again so I can start the *Shared Blessings Fund* to help those who are in dire need (like I have been so many times) when I learned to be quiet and quit blathering, I now hear back "If you want to be a millionaire again, then use the gifts I have already given you." It is said with all the love in the world and makes me realize again that we all have been given the gifts and tools we need to change our lives and make them be anything we want them to be. I certainly have a ton of God-given talents and ideas...and the ability to make them work. I have all the "Faith" (in God) in the world, but another thing I have learned in my ups and downs is that you also need Trust, which I also happen to have in abundance...thank God.

Faith in God is easy for most of us, but completely and honestly trusting Him; well, that's another matter altogether. How many times do we all ask God for something, wait for it to happen or not happen, as the case may be, and when the waiting becomes intolerable we take matters into our own hands? How many times do we ignore the fact that sometimes "No" IS an answer? When things do not happen as you planned or would like, down the road you will be thanking God that it did not happen, and what did happen replaced it. His plan for us is always even better than anything we could begin to imagine...if we would just have the patience, faith and trust in Him and know things will work out to our benefit.

How many times in our lives do we forget that there is a time and a season for everything, and things happen in God's time, not necessarily in ours...no matter how much we think it would be the right thing? Do you think God is not listening to you? He is, at all times. Do you think that God doesn't care about your issues? He does care, and He shows His caring and His love for you all day every day. If you learn to trust that God *is* there and He *is* paying attention to your needs and issues, life gets a LOT smoother. When you realize all the magic and miracles that DO happen in your day, you not only know that He is aware of you, but also know that you can trust that He has your well being foremost in His mind...always.

Some people say God is judgmental and vengeful. I don't believe that for a minute. I believe that He is patient, kind, loving and understanding. He knows that we don't all "get it" at the same time. How boring would that be? He knows that if one person gets His message and shares it with others, and they share it with others, His word will eventually be spread throughout the world. Any message, personally delivered by someone, makes a much larger impact than general message to all. He knows that when one person recognizes the gifts He gave them and is willing to encourage others to see and use their own gifts, the world will change—one person at a time. He is patiently waiting...giving us His faith and trust that we will learn, understand, and make it happen.

When you see someone successfully using the gifts they have been given, you will also be seeing a person who not only has faith, but also has learned to leap off that cliff and trust that God has them in His sights, that God IS paying attention and things *will be okay.* This is exactly the kind of person that you need to approach and ask for time to discuss *your* gifts and how you might use them. They will make time for you. It's part of their gift. You will need to acknowledge that these are busy people, and it may be by e-mail or phone that they can talk to you, but if you ask for their help they will most likely fit you into their schedule. If you get someone in your sights and they are not receptive (I have been ignored, found others plain rude, and been totally blown off many, many times), you have approached the wrong person. They are not in the space you are shooting for, and it is another blessing from God that they did not make time for you. Everything does happen (or not happen) for a reason, and you will be lead to the right person to help you if you pay attention to all of the people you meet.

It takes a special person to not only have faith in God, but to learn to *always* trust in His presence, His awareness of you and your well being, and His love for us all. YOU ARE THAT SPECIAL PERSON. It may take a little trial and error to get the hang of it, but when you learn to completely and honestly trust that the Spirit of God is within you, you are on your way to wherever you want to be.

If there is one thing I have learned, it's that there is NO LIMIT to what anyone can accomplish if they let God work through them and remain at peace. I am currently working on a Community Outreach Program that will benefit kids in need. God planted this seed of an idea in me because He knew that He also gave me the ability to make a difference in many children's lives by making it work. Then He kept nudging me about it until I got with the program and took steps to make it happen. Again, He provided me with the angels to help in Tammy, and Pastor Chris James and a couple of local business men and women that truly care.

I think it sometimes feels like we are being tested. That feeling is in our heads…a reason why things might not go as planned, a convenient excuse. I do not believe that God has the time, energy or inclination to test us. Testing is not what He is about. I believe the spirit of God is just begging to work through us to share all the love, kindness, joy and peace, and abundance that are what He is. You'll hear it if you listen. Will you allow Him to work through you to reach others?

Remember this: If a thought comes to mind and you ignore it, and it keeps coming to mind…it is a message to you to use one of the gifts you have been given. If you are willing to do the legwork, and will *trust* God to take care of the rest, it will work out okay in the end. That does not mean there will be no obstacles, it just means that you can and will overcome them or find a way around them if you try hard enough. It may not happen exactly when and how you thought it would, but it will happen when and how it is supposed to if you have patience. It all boils down, as always, to having faith AND trust that God really is paying attention to you and He knows what He is doing.

Finding YOUR Gifts

We all have gifts that we can share with others. The nice thing about these gifts is that you can find them at any age. Your gifts may be in the business world, in the home, in arts and crafts, in writing, working with children, the elderly, or people more disadvantaged than you. The possibilities are endless. How do you find your true gifts? Start by making lists. No rush. Make them, review and revise them as much as you want, as this is just for you.

Make a list of people in your everyday life. Family, friends, people you work with, and acquaintances. Now write down next to each name several things you think they are good at. If you were to share your opinion with them, they would probably be surprised...you might want to do that. We all need to hear what someone else thinks we are good at once in a while. Try to think of things that are not totally obvious. A professional at something being good at it is not what we are looking for, like a professional hockey player that can skate well. It's the little things in life that they do on a daily basis, or skills they have like singing or teaching, making people smile...this list will limber you up without focusing on yourself right away.

Now make a list of the things you think *you* are good at. You might want to ask around and see if anyone has anything to add to your list that you might not have considered. Let it sit overnight. Review it and add other things you thought of while getting dressed or driving. Take your time and make sure you really have a good list. Now cross off anything that you do NOT enjoy doing. Just because you are good at something does not mean you enjoy it. I am good at cleaning my house, but I don't like to do it.

Your third list is a list of things that you do or would enjoy. It could be gardening, singing, writing, golf or any other sport, reading, cooking, sewing or crocheting, hunting or fishing, photography, browsing the internet, travel, working with people, or any number of things. This list is not necessarily of things that you are good at, just that you have an interest in. You may never have done something on this list. If you have an interest in it, could learn to do it, and thinking about that makes you smile, then it goes on the list. Put a star next to anything that you are also good at.

To follow your dream and feel like you are purposefully using your gifts, what you do has got to be something you do well or can learn to do well, but also something you thoroughly enjoy. Think of people you know who motivate you, or you admire for their enthusiasm for what they are doing. They obviously enjoy what they do and also are good at it or they would not have made an impression on you.

A checker at the grocery store can either obviously like their job or obviously just be putting in their time for the paycheck. If you are smiling after waiting in a long line, the card swiper doesn't work right, and there is no bagger so it takes longer, then that checker is using his or her gift of personality and love of people to make your experience a little better. They are good at their job and love working with people. It does not have to be earth-shattering science, it just has to be something you enjoy and are good at, or could learn to do well.

If you pay attention as you go through your day, you will notice those who are using gifts they have been given to make another person's day a little brighter. But how many times a day do you consciously notice that, or anything else, about the person at the fast food place, your co-workers, or anyone that just crosses your path? Generally we are so wrapped up in our own day that we don't notice others one way or the other.

Sit down at the end of any given day and make a list of every person who crossed your path that day, then write down what gift they shared with you. It could be a smile, a hello, assistance with whatever you were doing at the time, directions, advice, a kind word, or an idea…

It could be someone gossiping, or acting mean or angry, that gave you the gift of a reminder to not participate in that type of unbecoming behavior. The negative behavior in others always affords us the opportunity for forgiveness and unconditional love in response, which is a good gift to put at the top of your list.

Put a star next to anyone that made your day a little brighter. Put two stars next to those to whom you returned the favor.

If you admire people who have the gift of gab, there are groups you can join to make you more comfortable speaking in front of others. If you admire people who can just whistle around a computer, there are places you can go to learn computer skills. With any subject and a little investigation on your part there is always a place you can find to improve the skills you need to go forth and share you gift with others. Again, it must be something that you do or would enjoy. My sister Althea is the queen of home décor, sewing and making crafty things. I admire her for that. I could easily find classes and learn to do those types of things, and do them well…but I would not enjoy it nearly as much as other things that I am interested in. That's why I have a sister with those talents!

You have a choice to make. So far, your life has gone along and it can continue in the same way, for the rest of your life, if you choose. If you feel that there has just got to be more to life, or that you are not using your God-given gifts to the fullest, then changes need to be made. This does not mean that you have to completely switch jobs, move to another part of the country, or anything drastic. It just means that you must wake up and smell the roses, be determined to become aware of what your personal gifts are...and to find a way to share them with others on a daily basis. You don't have to share every gift on a daily basis, but at least one every chance you get.

If you want your life to change, you have to consciously commit to making the necessary changes. Please note that while you are thinking about your gifts you are not thinking about the pile of laundry that needs done, what so and so said to so and so at work, what the mechanic just told you was wrong with your car or anything else on the usual unending list of things to address in your daily life. Your thoughts have been positive and, hopefully, enthusiastic about changes you can personally make to create a more fulfilling next chapter of your life, which starts NOW. This is a good frame of mind, and a great space to be in. It can be what every day is like for you if you decide that's what you need and want, and it's much better than the alternative.

Identifying your personal gifts is one thing, but then what? What do you do with that information? You've got it...make a list! We'll start with the last list of things that interest you.

On your new list, transfer the things you would enjoy doing *and* you are, or could be, good at. Leave plenty of space between items. Now write next to them how you might share that gift with others. This is another list that will take days, if not weeks, to complete. We'll call this one our "Master List" (you can put the others away). You might want to ask others for ideas of how you could expand on that gift.

An item on this list might be something that all of your friends or family keeps telling you to do something with. Those are messages you should be listening to. If you keep having a thought over and over of something new that you do, or could learn to do well, that is the message you are looking for. We are so busy getting through our days and weeks the way they are, the additional effort it would take to implement something new is at times overwhelming. But don't forget...*then there you are.*

If you want things to change in your life, you have to be willing to put in the effort. When you keep hearing something over and over again, then it is meant for you to pay attention to, not to shove under your mental rug or ignore. I have several items that need addressing, this book being one of them, which I have just kept putting off for several years until "the right time," when I could afford to just sit and write, or had the money to do something. I finally decided that if I just do what I am being urged to do I will be able to afford anything. I find or make the time to write now...not later. If you are focused on accomplishing something new, it is amazing how the things that you used to spend (waste) time doing don't even matter anymore. That part of life goes on its merry way without you, and soon you begin to wonder what the fascination with all of those things was in the first place?

Now we go back to our Master List. If you have several things on your list, you probably cannot implement them all at the same time. Keep in mind that we are looking for new ways to use our God-given gifts and share them with others. This will, in turn, make your life more fulfilled and benefit all those you are able to share your gifts with. Review your options on the Master List with these questions in mind:

> -Does this benefit just me, or will it make a difference in other people's lives? Being the entrepreneur that I am, I have started several major projects that, for one reason or another (usually lack of money) did not work out. As I look back on those things now, they would have made *me* and the manufacturers a lot of money, but would not have benefited anyone else. One thought is that if you create a product, you create jobs (impacting others lives in a good way), but guess what? Those workers have plenty of work without my new

whatjamagidgget. I have learned to make that a consideration in my choices and things seem to work out better. That does not mean things just fall into place, but they do get better results in the end. And I find it so much more rewarding to actually be involved with projects that can positively affect even one other person's life.

-Does it seem like the same things keep happening in your life over and over, and you can never get beyond them to where you want to be? I have felt like that so many times. I believe that is because we are given the same situation time and time again until we learn that lesson and get it right. I have always been a slow learner in that respect. I am the queen of "Well, if that doesn't work, I'll try this...then that...then something else." Things not working out do not faze me because I always have the next plan in my sights. Not a good program, by the way. It's better to figure out the lesson, learn it and then move on.

Until this past year I never realized that I must stop...and evaluate what it is that keeps happening, and how I *always* respond. If I am totally quiet and paying attention, not to what I usually think about something, but what my new gut feeling about it is, then I have my answer. Usually one that I have thought about, been told about, felt and ignored time and time again. Instead of just thinking, "okay, I'll do it this way, and if it doesn't work out, I'll think of something else" this time I move forward with a knowing that I have made the right choice. It's a choice I can believe in and a feeling of trust that I am finally on the right path...by the grace of God.

-Is it something I know how to do, or do I need to research and learn to do it well? Not a show stopper. During the time it takes to research a subject and practice or learn how to do it well, your focus is will be on doing something that will benefit others some day. This focus will make a difference in every one of your days that it takes to make that happen. It is utterly amazing that when your focus is not all about yourself, your issues, and your needs and wants that life really does seem different...better and full of hope, love and happiness that you can share with others.

It is a rude awakening when you finally realize that life is not meant to be all about you. It is meant to be all about others, and what you can do for them by being a better you.

-What am I going to have to give up to make this happen? There is no free lunch, folks. Unless you are currently a major "couch potato," your day is probably pretty full from morning until night. If you think about the things you do in your day, some are mandatory, but others could be eliminated without major consequences. You have to be willing to make time for this endeavor, and if you don't...well then, there you are. Still.

Tips for squeezing productive time out of your day:

Driving: What do you do while driving? Are you thinking of the conversation you are going to have with someone in the future, or rehashing one from the past? Are you planning or re-planning what you are going to wear someplace? Are you gossiping on the phone with a friend because you are both bored while driving? Are you worrying about something that happened or is going to happen to you or someone else in your life or someone they know? So, how do you feel when you arrive? Tense, wound up, scattered?

STOP ALL OF THAT. Stay in the present moment and be thankful for everything you experience. Practice this for one day, then another: Be thankful for a vehicle to drive, or a bus to take, or the person giving you the ride. Notice the weather and how it affects the trees, bushes and the roads (driving). Notice the beautiful sky and be thankful for the amazing scenery. Carefully notice your surroundings that you would not notice if you were not aware in the moment. They build entire strip malls and I never knew they were there...for a year or two!

At a stop light, just be peaceful in the moment and thankful for that moment of peace. Being all upset that you are hitting every light, or the drivers in front of you are driving slowly will not make your journey any faster. Take that time to be thankful you are not walking. You will arrive when you arrive. If being late is an issue, then make it a non-negotiable point with yourself to leave earlier. No excuses.

Once you get the hang of peaceful driving time, you will be able to spend some of it thinking about your gifts you are going to share with whomever you are going to see when you arrive. If you want to think about something, what better thing could there be to plan?

This can be anything from a smile for everyone, no matter who you see, to helping someone with a project they are working on, listening to someone who needs to talk, teaching someone something they have a hard time with, changing the subject when others start to gossip, to just sharing your joy for life with all others. Most people you see in your day are, unfortunately, not in a joyful space at that moment. They are just hanging out and hanging on...trying to get through the day and week. If your goal is nothing other than to get in a joyful space while driving and spread it around all day, then you are giving a great gift to each and every person that crosses your path. You don't have to get nutsy about it. Just quietly be happy and joyful, calm and peaceful. It will make their day better, even if they don't realize why.

Setting Boundaries: Wow, you can squeeze a lot of time out here. How many conversations do you have in your day just to have them? If you pay attention throughout the day, there will be many that just waste time. Notice how many conversations you had today that didn't change anything, fix anything, or make a difference to anything. You and someone else were just talking. Or one of you were ranting and raving about a perceived injustice. Talk about time wasters! I used to spend a large portion of my day doing just that, on both ends of the stick.

Useless conversations (those not about sharing pertinent information, making plans to do something positive or enjoyable, or discussing something pertinent to both of you) are taking up your valuable and limited time. Time spent that you can never get back. Time you could put to good use.

The phone: Most of the time we call until we reach the one of our "best friends" that actually answers the phone, explain a situation in way more detail than is necessary, give our point of view and wait to hear total confirmation that we did or said just the right thing. Of course this should be immediately followed by our friend with a thorough trashing of the person who did or said that dastardly thing we just described. Then we can get on to the business of talking about work (and everyone there) and the kids (and their friend's/parents/teachers) and the rest of the family or friends. Hellloooo?

Practice this for one day, then another: NO time wasting phone calls over two minutes. Use all that extra time to do something productive and positive toward sharing your gifts with others. Excuse yourself politely by saying that you are sorry, but you have some work to do. Use the rest of that half hour or hour you would have spent on the phone to do, or plan to do, something using your God-given gifts. By the way, if you just sit down and watch TV, you might as well have stayed on the phone.

At home: At my home, the rules have changed. My friends have always known that if they had a problem, I had an answer.

They were always welcome to come over to talk about it. They were usually upset about something and would arrive in an absolute state. They would sit down and go on and on (and on and on and on) about whatever happened. We would cuss it and discuss it every which way to Sunday. Throughout this I would give them my sage advice. I have to admit that I would always ask God to give me whatever He wanted them to know, and I would say it. Most of it was exactly the opposite of what they wanted to hear, and not necessarily agreeing with their take on the situation. Over the years, my friends have learned just about what I will say, and they stay away if they don't want to hear it. That makes me laugh, but they know I won't just say what they want to hear.

Then it dawned on me what a waste of time those hours upon hours were. What I said made sense to them, but when they left they did exactly what they wanted and would have done without any input on my part. So, the point was? Just to vent I suppose, and loving them all as I do, they now usually call someone else to share that with. I am not receptive to those types of lengthy conversations any more. That does not mean I don't care...if it is a new situation (rare) or crisis, I am there. Not for the same song, 85th verse, not anymore. My time, and my choice.

Not long ago a young friend, Ashlee, was staying at my house for a week. The first day, she came flying in the door all wound up about something someone else had done and said. I could tell she was about to go off on a lengthy tangent about what happened and I stopped her in her tracks. I made her be quiet, take a deep breath and asked her what she noticed? She was bewildered, so I mentioned that she should notice how peaceful it was standing there in my kitchen. I informed her that we would not be disturbing the peace in my home by ranting and raving about something that was (1) not about her (2) something she couldn't fix or change (3) something that would not be affected at all by her being upset about it...the people actually involved wouldn't know or care. I told her that she would have to do that stuff somewhere other than in my home. She laughed and agreed.

We talked at length during her stay about creating a peaceful life and staying there no matter what others were doing. I told her to draw an imaginary box around herself and always keep it in mind. If someone was doing or saying something irrelevant or not "her thing" she had a choice not to let it get dumped in her box. When you get in the habit of thinking to yourself, "that's nice, but don't dump it in my box, it's not about me or "my thing," your life becomes so much more peaceful. If it's not in your box, you don't have to deal with it, and since it's not your thing anyway, that saves wasted time. On and off through the week she would start to go off on something and I would quietly ask, "Is that your thing?" and she would say, "No, and I should get it out of my box." We laughed, and she was getting the hang of it.

Toward the end of the week, Ashlee's friend came over and they were sitting on one couch with me on the other. I was, as usual, on my laptop and they were just talking girl talk. Her friend started to get wound up and was about to say something trashing another girl and Ashlee stopped her immediately. Ashlee told her friend that they couldn't do that in my house, they would have to go outside to do that (true story). Of course, her friend had no idea what Ashlee was talking about, so she explained that we don't talk about other people's things and issues in my house; it disturbs the peace. I am absolutely sure that friend thought we were both nuts, but she did not continue with whatever rant she was about to share with us. We had a peaceful rest of her visit, with Ashlee and me grinning at each other off and on.

How much time do you spend in your home listening to someone talking about someone other than themselves? Your kids may be telling you about a teacher or another child at school. Your spouse or significant other, if you have one, may be talking about people at work or a meeting. You yourself may be talking about people in your day. And don't forget the never-ending phone calls to share the day's events with others. Look at all the time spent on issues that really don't belong in your box to begin with. I know we all want to be kept in the loop with what is going on in the world of our friends and family, but this could and should be a very limited amount of our time, and positive in nature.

What if you took that same time and talked with another person about THEIR activities in the day; how THEY handled a situation, or might have handled it differently; about YOUR or THEIR accomplishments and successes? Maybe pointing out how normal events *were* an accomplishment or success of THEIRS, helping you to realize normal events that were a personal success of YOURS? Those things all belong in your box. They are about you and, or the person you are talking to directly. You are focused on, listening to and showing your interest in THEM. What a very good use of time, and an irreplaceable gift from you to them. You might talk about goals, both short and long term, ideas, plans or anything that pertains to who is in the discussion at the time. There is limited time wasted on people and situations that are about someone else, time to use on your gifts.

Remember that if you can't fix it or change it, if your worrying, being upset or discussing it will make no difference to the situation or the other person involved, it is NOT YOUR THING and does not belong in your box. Time saved by this can really add up, and be time used to work on sharing your gifts.

In Public: Work is a given, as are: the grocery store, Target or whatever, church if you attend and participate, the cleaners, school events and sports team events. There are certain places we must or choose to go, but that does not mean that we have to let others dump their stuff in our box while we are there. That is always a personal choice on your part, and you can stand or sit there listening to others' laments, and details of issues, and others…or not.

Instead of avoiding someone or asking, "How are you?" to someone you know will give you a lengthy description of their current illnesses or issues and status of each, learn to ask a yes or no question. "Are you having a good day?" If they say yes, you can briefly explore what is good about it. If they say no, you can reply with something like, "Oh, something good must have happened today," and encourage them to think of one good thing. If they can't, you can always end it by saying, "I always consider it a good day when I wake up," which generally will lead them to agree. If nothing else, tell them that in that case they surely need a hug…and give them one. Anyone having that bad of a day definitely needs a hug. We all need hugs. Then you can politely move along…you shared a gift with them, back to your own things.

Then there are places we regularly go that just take up time. Giving these up is also a personal option. It may be a meeting in the middle of your day that you do not get any benefit from, but are in the habit of going to. Maybe you stop somewhere on the way home, just to be sociable, probably staying way longer than you planned on. Perhaps you are single, or the family is busy, and you are in the habit of going to the local bar(s) at night, instead of the dreaded "staying home alone" option. I have done all of these. I chose not to continue, but, again, that is a personal choice. I came to the conclusion that time wasted in those type of situations was MUCH better spent at home, reading or doing something to benefit me and my goals in life. Or just spoiling myself with a long hot bubble bath (*real men* do take bubble baths, by the way). If you don't take time to spoil you, why should anyone else? That's my theory.

I have so many friends that desperately "want their lives to change and be better," but will not even consider giving up their meaningless social life to make that happen. They are not willing to do what it takes to change anything about their life, which is fine, and their choice...but all I can say to them is, "then there you are."

There are a lot of ways to change your life, but you have to be willing and ready to make it happen. Looking and waiting for someone else to make your life different or better is not the answer. You usually have a fun beginning, then just more of the same.

So now you have hopefully taken your "Master list" and thought about what gifts you would enjoy sharing with others, if you are not already doing so. You have decided what you can do well, or could learn to do well, and how you might turn that into something you can share. You have considered where you might find the time to make these changes in your life.

Now, here comes your biggest choice of all...whether to keep hanging out and hanging on like most folks, or to take charge of this new chapter of your life and make it different, better, so much more fulfilling and rewarding. You cannot begin to imagine the difference in a day that is focused on others and what you can do for them, instead of "what's in it for me?" or worse yet, just going through the motions to get the day over with...until you try a day that is all about others. Practice this for one day, then another.

If what you have chosen on your Master List is something you are serious about, but you are not *quite* ready to jump right on it, or make the time for *right* now, please consider some other options that are always available to you to share in your normal day. They are things that we all have in our God-given bag of tricks, they are always available, and will get you in the spirit of giving:

Kindness - when are you too busy to be kind?
Joy - sharing joy with others lifts you up at the same time

Peacefulness - answer turmoil, or anger, by remaining calm and peaceful, and watch the difference in the situation.
Understanding - give the understanding to others that you want for yourself
Forgiveness - we expect God to forgive us, how can we not forgive others?
Unconditional love - learn to accept people how and where they are in life.

All of these things are given to us in unending abundance, so there is no excuse not to pay them forward, so to speak. By regularly sharing these types of gifts with your family, friends, co-workers, acquaintances, and strangers alike, you will realize that you are also sharing…the grace of God.

Getting from Here to There

I'm not going to sugar coat it; this can be a very hard row to hoe. It not always easy, and not always a barrel of laughs, but if you make a commitment to yourself to change this next chapter of your life, then you only have yourself to answer to.

This personal journey may have peaks and valleys, mountain after mountain to climb, but it will also have the *most incredible* results if you stay with it and accomplish your goals…whatever they may be. The bigger your new goals, the more challenging it may be. Whenever you get disillusioned, disappointed, or you wonder if it is worth it, just sit quietly and picture it already being the way you want it to be and notice the peacefulness that vision provides. That should give you the encouragement to start back on your journey and complete it, making your life and the lives of all that you touch more meaningful, joyful and full of God's love.

Start where you are. Again, sit quietly and think about your life and the things you are determined to change. See the new chapter and what each day will be like. Plan in where you can share your gifts, large or small, with others. Enjoy that vision and KNOW that it can be so. Thank God (or the Universe, Spirit, whatever you believe in) for accompanying you on your journey, guiding you and helping you to attain your goals. Think of the others your journey will benefit in the end.

I like to call my personal journey my *Spiritual Quest*. I personally believe that we are all Spirit (of God) in this body for this lifetime on earth. I have come to believe that we are not our body, what we do, or what we have in the way of material possessions. We are here to share God's love, kindness and joy with others. Each of us will accomplish that (or not) in our own way, and that is as it should be. I believe that is our true purpose, and anything we add, by using our God-given gifts, is frosting on the cake.

I have always been friendly and nice to all people, no matter their station in life at the time. I was raised that way. I always got along with almost everyone I chose to...but I never choose a lot of people as close friends. I spend a lot of time alone (compared to most people I know) and that is okay with me. I always say "I play well alone," and mean that in a good way. I have always been comfortable in my own company, even though I grew up with siblings and lots of friends of all kinds.

Last night, I went to dinner alone at a local restaurant. When we are at a restaurant, we usually order, eat and leave without noticing the other people, unless to judge or criticize. Last night I took the time to sit there and notice each of the wait staff, all of the customers and other staff I saw. It was amazing to consciously realize that if we are all Spirit (of God) in these bodies, then we are all connected by that Spirit. Each one of us, wherever we go, is connected to every other person through God's Spirit. I sat there thinking about each person in my line of sight at the time...wondering who they were and what their story was? It reminded me how many times I have read the quote of Mother Teresa when she said that she loved to see God in all His different disguises. All shapes, sizes, color, attitudes and personalities and stations in life are different. The one thing we all have in common, however, is God's unconditional love for us, His Spirit in us and working through us, and His gifts that we have to share with others. Deciding to use those gifts is a personal decision. Finding or making a way is your own personal journey, and age is not a factor.

We all start out in a valley or on a plateau of some sort just because it is where we are.

No matter where you are now, there are higher places ahead, whether they are foothills or mountains to climb. When you feel you have accomplished a goal, you should be looking for the next challenge that is the continuation of your journey.

Mile Markers - Part One

> You know you are in a valley when (this is not a redneck joke)...
>
> - Things do not go smoothly, as you envisioned.
> - It takes much longer than you thought to accomplish your goals.
> - People do not think your idea will work—and are happy to tell you so.
> - People do not return phone calls when you leave messages about your idea.
> - People do not, in general, respond as favorably as you thought they would.
> - People keep telling you to do something else with your time.
> - People's eyes glaze over when you are talking about your idea.
> - People tell you what you should do instead (everyone has an opinion).
> - You feel beaten down by negative attitudes and response

Just keep on keeping on. You have a gift. You want to share that gift with others. You just haven't talked to enough people or the right people. It's in the numbers, and you have to have a certain amount of no's. Say thank you, and mean it, when someone says no or the equivalent thereof. Tell them you understand (knowing they are just not the right person) and thank them for considering your idea. You are getting the no's out of the way up front, which is not a bad thing. Lack of immediate success gives you practice, and the opportunity to make something even better than you had originally planned. You might streamline or add to your plan…never a bad thing to have review time. Always look for the good in what you thought was a bad thing…it's there, you just have to figure out what it is. In the end it always turns out that these are blessings in disguise. When you look at it that way, it is not traumatic, but just another step in the learning process. See it that way and move on.

This is where, quite honestly, the best chance to give up occurs. "Well, if no one else is interested, and no one cares, then it is probably a stupid idea that won't work." NOT SO. If you have truly and honestly thought this through and it is a gift you can and are willing to share, then keep on trucking. This is not about how other people see your idea or efforts…it is about YOU, and you sharing YOUR gifts. Maybe you need to look at your approach and change some things? Perhaps you could choose a more receptive group to approach? Everything happens, or doesn't, for a reason. It could just be timing. It could be that your idea will lead you to something even better, that you are good at and didn't realize it. This is not a stopping point, it is an evaluation point.

While you are evaluating, reach out to others any way you can. That will change your focus and clear your mind. All of a sudden the answers you were missing will seem as clear as day. The people or things you needed to continue, or improve, your original plan will show up…by the grace of God. The valley doesn't seem so bad, when you finally realize you are not alone on this journey.

I feel like I am again in one of these valleys right now, this minute. My answer is not to give up, but to realize that success is right around the corner. If I believe that with all my heart, then I will automatically do what it takes to move forward. I know that for a fact. I needed a little pick-me-up, so I decided to write some more. By re-reading this book from the beginning, it gave me exactly what I needed to stay the course, in spite of EVERYONE else's opinion that I should do something else instead of working on my ideas. It's how I feel about it that counts. Not my family, not my friends or acquaintances, but my own view of the situation. I don't just think...I KNOW that I am doing what I should be doing, using my creativity and working to bring projects that help others to fruition. As much as I love them, other's opinion is not "my stuff" and I will consider their input, but in the end, I will depend on my faith, trust and *knowing* that I AM on the right track.

Let me tell you about a valley so you won't be caught off guard. One side of the valley (the one you arrived from) is full or fear, doubt, confusion and panic. It seems like nothing is ever going to go right and you don't know what to do next.

If you have another or additional income in the household, then it is not quite as frightening as it is frustrating. If what you are trying to accomplish just isn't going the way you planned and is taking longer than you thought, you are in the valley to wander to the peaceful center of the valley, become peaceful and learn a better or more effective way of accomplishing your goals. Then you are able go to the other side, to choose your next mountain and start climbing.

For the many, like me, who don't just slide into the valley, but take a giant leap of faith (financially) and have landed there it is a whole different experience. It can be a rough landing, and a temporarily scary experience. It's like something popped a hole in your hot air balloon and you did a free-fall to the ground. You also land in the area with all the fear, doubt, confusion and panic...but you jump right up and immediately venture farther into the valley. Wandering around, usually in total confusion as to what you did wrong (not realizing you are just in the wrong frame of mind), you find the peaceful center and sit down for a while to think, to listen and to learn. Going forward with the exact same plan is probably not the answer, but you need some help with the correct approach.

The valley is where you get the choice to quit, or learn and go forward. What you have to learn is determined on where you are in life, and where you are trying to get to. The only journey I can tell you about is mine, as they are all individual journeys.

I have HUGE goals and, therefore, a harder row to hoe. My dream is to really be able to help others financially, and for that I apparently had a long way from where I was to where I needed to be. That happens sometimes. In addition to personal improvement (and lots of it), I am single and have to produce an income at the same time...easier said than done, to someone like me. Instead of finding a "sugar daddy" to support me while I learn and write, I trust that God would prefer I have faith in Him, and it works.

Okay, things do get shut off from time to time (all things in God's time, not ours), but I always find a way to get the important things (like basic bills) paid eventually. I have said, "God never gives you more than you can handle and then He gives you the strength to handle it," and He does. He gives you nerves of steel when you need them most. I have said that everything does (or does not) happen for a reason, and every time something less than favorable ("BAD!") has happened in the past five or so years, I think about helping others, and this is part of my learning curve. It gives me a different perspective on life and the strength to endure and go on. It increases my faith and trust in God each time adversity appears. I *know* I will succeed...by the Grace of God, and He knows I know.

I didn't used to see it that way. Bankruptcy, eviction, utilities shut off, rolling pennies to get gas and milk, and all the other situations that go along with *no money* were just bad things to overcome. I did not evaluate why they happened to me...I just dealt with them, overcame the current situation and moved on and up. These past five years have brought some of the same scenarios to my life again, but now I know why...so I know, first-hand, what being in these types of situations is like and how to overcome them and share that with you. This time, it is not about my survival, my life or anything to do with me. God gave me the ability to share those experiences and encouragement to overcome them with others...that would be you.

If you asked any of my good friends over the past five years, I believe they would say about me that I always, no matter the circumstance, have enough blind faith for twenty people...then they would probably tell you what stupid choices they think I make. Not to worry. I have always had that kind of faith (in God) that He had a plan for me and things would work out. I just was never sure exactly what the plan was, but I knew He did, and I was willing to be there to follow His plan. That has been my problem all those years. I had faith, but it was blind faith.

I feel like the blind man in the Bible, and God was waiting for me to figure things out for all these years; but when I didn't do it on my own, He finally plunked me firmly back in the valley and made sure that I knew that the answer lie in a different kind of faith, and He has (lovingly) given me the time to do the research and find it. I feel like running around shouting, "I can see!" and I get it now. I have learned through these experiences that God *is* paying attention and He *will* get your attention if you don't get, or ignore, His messages. He will go to whatever length it takes to get you with the program, when He feels your time to "get it" and share it with others. No matter how good your plan is, it won't work unless you incorporate His message to you in it. Nothing in your awakening will hurt you, but it will sure get your attention...trust me, I know.

I am a voracious reader, and that has been my path to better understanding. Sometimes it may be a speech you hear or a presentation of some sort that helps you see the light. I had messages from many people along the way, but did not know enough to pay attention to them…silly me. I now look for those messages everywhere.

In another valley (at another time) I used to read things like *The One Minute Millionaire,* and *Millionaire Next Door* to help me find answers. They weren't there. I read *The Four Agreements* by Don Miguel Ruiz, then everything else he wrote. They were helpful as a person, but not the answer. For a long time I was very focused on his principals of being impeccable to my word, not taking things personally, not making assumptions and doing my best at things, but life did not change dramatically, other than I was a much better person for it. It was progress, but I still had a long way to go.

In this particular valley (now), I have read *The Game of Life, and How to Play It* by Florence Scovel Shinn. Good book. *Your Best Life Now* by Joel Osteen. I read Michelle McKinney Hammond's *What to Do Until Love Finds You,* in which she reminds us that God has a person in mind for each of us. If we singles would stop trying to shove square pegs in round holes long enough to let Him bring us together with His chosen mate for us, He would be happy to do that. And, in the meantime, Michelle advises to let God be the person in your life. After all, He doesn't complain, criticize, get angry or judgmental…He is patient, kind, loving, understanding, and full of joy at all times. He is a great provider, AND He has a great sense of humor. What more could you ask for? I then read almost everything else Michelle had written. Michelle is a faith-based author, and writes mostly about single women and their lives. I love her books, and have many of them.

My favorite author, and I like to think "mentor for the moment" (unbeknownst to him), is Dr. Wayne Dyer. His books are amazing. For years and years my mom would tell me to read *Erogenous Zones* for one reason or another. It is Wayne's first book, but I would never read it as she suggested. The message was there, over and over, but I didn't pay attention...silly me. It wasn't my time to read it.

My friend brought over *Power of Intention* by Wayne (I call him Wayne, as I have spent *so many* hours reading his thoughts) and she set it on my coffee table. It was not until I had finished all of Michelle's books I had that I picked it up and read it just because I thought I should. (Learning to pay attention to messages) What an amazing day that was. I can read a book in a day, so I went to the library and got every book of his I could find. I couldn't mark in them, though, so as soon as I could squeak out the money I bought his books (or some he suggested) as I could, to read, mark up, read and read again...which I have done. I considered it an investment in myself. I just reread several again this past weekend. If you want his books you can buy them, borrow them (not from me, I have marked them all up) get them from the library or go to http://www.drwaynedyer.com. Most of his things are also on tape if you are not a reader. I am not going to go into what they say specifically, but I will share with you the difference they made for me.

Another fantastic book (recommended by Wayne) is *Ask and it is Given* by Jerry and Esther Hicks. I carried this book around for months on end, and after hearing about it over and over, finally it dawned on me that I was actually supposed to sit down and read it. I have reread it many times, and have a "lending copy" on hand so I don't have to give mine out. A little different take on things, but it's on the same premise. *The Law of Attraction*, also by the Hicks, is my latest book read and reread...a must read for everyone.

Beliefs are personal and everyone has their own. Some beliefs we have carried over from childhood, perhaps our religious upbringing, or family and friends' beliefs that we don't analyze, we just claim. Unless you have an open mind, you generally cannot, or do not, accept beliefs that are new or different than yours. I was like that for most of my life, which is a BIG stumbling block to me getting on the right path for this new chapter in my life.

When you meet someone with beliefs (about anything) that differ from your own, you need to accept that person right where they are. You do not have to agree with their beliefs or condone them; you just need to accept that person, again, where they are. You can walk away, or you may choose to share your beliefs with them, and they are free to accept or reject your beliefs by accepting you right where you are. If everyone believed the same things, we would have no purpose here on earth. God is infinitely patient. He knows that sooner or later we will all get it right…each in our own time, and our own way.

I finally opened my mind to new things…heck, I was sitting in my latest valley, and not that busy, so why not try something new and different? Something had to work out better than what I had been doing for the past few years! I read all these books months ago and tried so hard to do all these new things that I felt compelled to do, but still something was missing. So I reread them all again and again. It's confusing when one book suggests this and another suggests that. You would have to have lists a mile long to review all day to keep it all straight. Then it dawned on me that if I just put it all together, I would find the answers I was looking for. It's not in a bunch of instructions from any author on how to change your life for the better, it's in a new way of being you that makes all the difference in the world. I'll write what I believe we are all to emulate, but if you want the why and how, you'll have to check with the experts. You may agree or disagree, but that's your beliefs, these are mine:

When my girlfriends and I talk about God (and we do), a couple of them always point or look up when they mention God. I know they are indicating God in Heaven, not on the ceiling or upstairs in my bedroom, but I believe that the Spirit of God is in everyone and everything. To me, He is not "up there somewhere," he is right here, right now, with me at all times, which makes it pretty convenient. I have been single eight years since my husband died, and now take Michelle's advice to heart...He is my guy for now, until He sends His choice for me to "fetch me." It is much more convenient just to talk to God right here than keep talking to the heavens and hope He hears me. Long distance is a hard way to have a good relationship, and my way works great.

My life has changed so much over the past year. I now wake up and the first thing I do is say good morning to Him (God) and ask how I may serve Him today? That's about as far as I can get until the fog lifts off my brain. After some coffee, I can think, so then I have my morning conversation thanking Him for the abundance in my life, saying the Prayer of Jabeze (another good book), and other things that pertain to my life now.

My goal is now to live "In Spirit" on a daily basis, which requires focus on *wanting* to live "In Spirit." I have to admit that I have tried and failed at most of this, but the light bulb finally went on this past weekend, and I know now that I am ready to do it every day, and that I can. Re-reading books lets you catch something you passed over the other times. I guess the right combination finally came up for me, and I feel like I won the lottery. I am so excited to go forward and use this precious gift I have been given, and to share it with others. Things I will now personally do differently:

1. Positive thinking at all times. Every time I catch myself thinking about what I need or don't have, I immediately switch it to thinking of how it feels to have it.

You attract what you think about, and if you dwell on scarcity, illness, sadness, fear, grief, anger, resentment, or anything else negative, then that is what you will get more of. I have had more than my share of all of those things, and I am willing to do what it takes to not have them included in this new chapter of my life...which means paying attention to my thoughts at all times.

I will focus on what I do want, and attract that to me, and give thanks daily for it's arrival. Many authors, my favorites and others, always say that you are what you think about. I will spend my days thinking good things and of positive results.

When I first ran out of money, I thought it would be temporary, as I had a plan that would make enough money to take care of the bills…I always do. But time after time, the plan of the moment wouldn't work out. I had no clue then that it was because I was always focused on what I lacked and I was bringing more of that need to me. When your focus is on what is going to be shut off next, or what bad thing will happen next, then you stay right there and have to deal with one issue after another. When you think of scarcity in your life, more scarcity is what you will have. I didn't know that then, but I sure do now.

When you focus on, and are thankful for, what you have (it's always abundance when compared to others with less) and you focus on the having more, then that is what will arrive. It's similar to the old, "if you want to be successful, act like you already are successful" theory. It's definitely not always easy to maintain, but it is doable, if you put your mind to it.

2. Think before I speak. When I pause and think *before* I speak or write an e-mail, it will remind me to decide *first* if what I say is positive, helpful, and encouraging to the other person?

Generally, I am supportive, always positive and almost always cheerful. But at the same time, in my adult life, I have spent a great majority of my conversational effort critiquing (and finding fault), judging (and finding others "wrong" in their choices, actions and deeds), criticizing (their wrongness), and deciding they should have done it differently (they way I think is right, of course).

I will now let everyone be who *they* are, where *they* are, and let them handle things the way *they* need to for where *they* are in *their* life. Their issues are not my issues, and don't belong in my box. I will listen, empathize, and help others review their options, but will not tell others what I think they should do, or should have done or said. I am sure I will be simply amazed as they manage their lives without me.

I have learned that critically judging anyone or anything only says that I am a person who needs to judge. I don't want to be that person anymore. I will view the world with compassion, understanding and acceptance.

Gossip is one of the hardest things to manage. You may have every intention of not gossiping with anyone about anyone else or anything, but boy, it's hard to actually do. That one will take some work and focus on an all-the-time basis, I can tell. My friend just called and I made it through without gossiping about anyone. Yahoo. Of course, I have been here writing for the past couple of days, so have not been anywhere or seen anyone to report about which helps. She had just been running errands, so had no input for the gossip mill, either, which also helped. And the phone call was relatively short. But lucking out is not the way to avoid gossiping. This weekend I figured out how to do that, too.

3. Give unconditional love to ALL. God gives us His unconditional love at all times, and I believe He expects us to pass it on to others. Not some others, but to all others. At all times.

We love our children "unconditionally," no matter what. We don't always have to like them, or approve of their choices in word, deed, (or music) etc., but we do love them because they are ours. We sometimes have to use "Tough Love" for their own safety, their own good or that of the family or community, and it could even go as far as having to temporarily turn our back on them, but we still love them. Good, bad or indifferent, they are our children no matter what.

Other family members, spouse or significant other, siblings, and good friends do not necessarily enjoy that automatic unconditional love. We are much more apt to love them if they behave this way or that, if they believe this or that, if they do or don't do this or that, and if they treat us as we think they should.

THEN we will love them "unconditionally"…well, as long as they continue as we think they should.

Then there are the co-workers, acquaintances and people we don't even know…friends or family of friends, co-workers of friends or family, strangers, on and on. These people certainly don't qualify for any kind of love from us, let alone unconditional love. Why not?

I have learned that each person is just as important as any other in this life. The Spirit of God is in all of us, so when we disrespect another in any way, shape or form, it is not only disrespecting ourselves at the same time, but it is showing disrespect for God. Okay, that brings me up short. I can't live "In Spirit" if I go around disrespecting others by being anything less than kind, polite, interested in them and willing to share the gift of love and joy with them that I have been given in abundance…by the grace of God.

Can you begin to imagine calling up a friend or family member and spending a half hour trashing God because this or that didn't go as you planned? Or you thought He would do this or that, but He didn't? "He said" this or that, but it didn't happen that way (however you interpreted what you were told "He said")? I can't. But that is, in effect, what we are doing when we gossip…trashing the God in us all. OUT with the gossip, and in with the love.

4. Remember that there are no mistakes. Every time I encounter someone or something, I will remember that they are in my life for a reason. If I don't acknowledge that fact, I will miss the gift or lesson I was supposed to get from that encounter; which is definitely my loss.

Many times we miss out on good things by not focusing on each person that crosses our path. Perhaps they are just an "extra" in our life, but most times they had something to share or offer us that we just ignored, or did not take the time to explore. How many times have you met someone and when you walked away wondered what you were told their name was? How many times have you just smiled and got back to what you were doing as quickly as possible? How many gifts have you missed? How many lessons have you not learned?

If someone does not provide a positive experience for you, they were then there to remind you of something or teach you a lesson (perhaps about yourself?), but they were there for a reason. You can walk away, but think of the reason, and learn from it.

I have many interests, but you would never know that if you didn't bother to ask and care about my answer. Some of those interests may be the same as yours, some may be something that you have always been interested in and would benefit from learning what I know about them, and some you would be less interested in, and hearing a short conversation about it may reinforce that for you (why reinvent the wheel?). But if you don't ask, and listen to the answer, you would never know any of that.

Asking how someone is and not listening to the answer, or caring what it was, is the usual way of doing business. Usually you just hope they say, "Fine" and leave it at that so you can talk about what you want to and get back to doing your own thing. Do you know anyone who always says, "Well, anyway"...and starts talking again every time you finish a sentence? I know several, and after the second or third time I usually try to remember not to offer an opinion or say much of anything at all so as not to interrupt them any further. Do you know anyone that says, "Whatever" after anything anyone else says, then starts talking? How much does that annoy you? It sure makes a statement...about them, not you. Many authors of assorted subjects will point out that most of the time people are not listening to someone else talk because they are forming their response or next opinion. How sad is that? But I am sure it is true. I have done it many times. NO more.

5. Turn things over to God...and LET GO. I had to work up to *knowing* that it was okay to let go. I thought it was, and I hoped

and prayed that it was. I tried to remember to let go, but that only lasted for so long.

I now know that it's okay to let go for as long as it takes Him to work things out (His way) to my benefit. It helps if the things you are letting go of are not specific to time and exact response. Things always do happen. Maybe not as you anticipated, or when you wanted or need them to, but in the end they are always to your benefit if you truly "Let go and let God." It's when you get impatient and try to do things yourself that they get messed up, not when He is in charge. Those were biggies for me to get the hang of.

You wouldn't put a load in the washer and pull it out five minutes later, mad because it isn't washed and spun and finish it by hand. You wait for it to wash and spin your clothes. You wouldn't put a two pound meat loaf in the oven and pull it out fifteen minutes later expecting to be able to eat it. You wait for it to bake. These types of things are a no-brainer. It just makes sense. You know how long they will take and have the patience (or sometimes just the sense) to wait until they are finished.

When your plan for life isn't working and, for whatever reason, you could be in jeopardy of losing all the material things in your life…possibly your home, would you be brave enough to say, "I'm willing to do that if needed, Lord. I trust you have my best interests at heart?" If you were about to lose your job, would you say that then? Would you trust that whatever happens will be in your best interest in the end? Not many are that brave or have that kind of trust that the road traveled will lead them where they need to go. Instead of panic and fear, you have to focus on faith and trust. Sometimes it's just something you have to learn. That's one lesson I have definitely learned.

I can, from experience, tell you that if the occasion ever does arise, if you are willing to let go of all that "matters" in your life, you may not have to. Just the fact that you are willing to take another "lesser or different" job, move to wherever you have to, or give up whatever you need to is what matters. I have come to this point several times in my life and lost some nonessential things along the way. But they were just things, and not what matters. At those times, I always think of Jesus walking the earth with nothing and doing God's work. I would be okay with just what is needed to do what I could for others, and following in His footsteps. I would be okay without all the "things and stuff' of life.

I have never gotten as far as having nothing, and I am grateful for my beautiful home, a vehicle that works and the things that make life comfortable. Because I would gladly let go of it all if needed, I haven't had to. I have a warm and safe place to learn and grow; to figure out the twists and turns of my life, and use them to help others possibly avoid the same things. If nothing else, to help others know that they are not alone and can make it through the tough times and succeed. To learn the answer is living "In Spirit" with God.

Living "In Spirit" is a whole different way of life. You have to be aware of these types of things (and more) all the time. Not just when you think of it, but throughout every day. I used to think that was a worthwhile, beneficial, but overwhelming job. I would try, but forget most of the day, then swear to try harder and do better tomorrow. Now I get it, and it's a breeze when you put it all together; what a joyful experience and way of life.

6. Staying in the present. Yesterday is done and gone, folks. You can't fix it, change it, make it different or better...it's over and done with. Spending much time in the past only takes time you could be using in the present. The future will be what it will be. It more depends on staying in the present than anything else. You can hope and dream, visualize and plan, but too much time there will never help you move forward.

There is a big difference in forming an idea and plan, visualizing it and staying with the feeling of accomplishing that goal and just sitting on the couch day after day pretending that it is reality. It is by staying in the present (in a positive and spiritually productive way), and taking one step at a time toward your goals, that they will be realized.

If the path turns out to be longer than you thought it would, you are tempted to think back to the past when things were easier, or spend your time longing for the future when your goals will have been accomplished. By doing either of those things, you are not seeing or appreciating the journey in the present, and are overlooking all the magic and miracles each day brings. And trust me when I say that every day does bring magic and miracles, whether it is in a person, place or thing, into your life. Looking for them, acknowledging them and appreciating them keeps you in the present, and helps you to make the best use of each and every day; not focused on those days, people and events that have been or *might* be.

How many conversations have you rehearsed in your mind and the situation you were going to use them in never came to pass? The right opportunity to "tell them what you thought" just did not present itself? You changed your mind, or what they said first totally took the wind out of your sails? How many hours, days or weeks did that rehearsal take? How many times have you thought of just the right thing to say all the way home, and shared that with a friend(s)? That can last for days and days, if you let it. What a waste of the present, since you can't get that time back and it doesn't change a thing.

You are probably grinning right now, like I am, at the thought of what some of those things, if said, would have produced. It's funny, now, but it probably wasn't then. I would have looked like an idiot (more than usual) if I would have said a portion of the things I had planned on in my life. And I spent a *lot* of time working that all out! I have spent hours upon hours rehashing situations in my mind and giving them different endings, had I just said this or that. Smart use of my time? I think not. No more!

If you do your best in the moment, and trust that you will do the same with whatever comes up, you do not have all the "what if's" to deal with, and can stay in the present in peace.

7. Take each day as it comes. I believe that every day is a new day, and we get a clean slate. If we mess up one day, it does not carry over into the next. Every time we awaken, we have a chance to have a good day and do it better, and get it right.

Yesterday was another good day. One of my best friends, Sheila, stopped over and we talked for a couple of hours. We discussed issues going on in our lives and helped each other think of ways to improve some things; we acknowledged and appreciated the good things in our lives. Twice I moved the topic along when she started going in a negative direction, and she switched immediately to something better. I do not remember gossiping once, so that put the frosting on the cake. Sheila is on her own spiritual quest at the moment, so it was easy to stay in a positive and productive place with her the whole time.

A year ago we would have (for sure) spent the entire time doing nothing more than talking about everyone in our lives, judging their actions, and announcing what they should have done. What a difference a year makes. What a difference spiritual awareness makes!

I had spilled some coffee on my laptop earlier (while rushing, when I didn't need to) and the only thing wrong with it now is the right arrow doesn't work. What a blessing is that? I found as couple of things I thought I had lost by being calm and patient in my search. They were not big things, but important to me at the time...another blessing for sure.

Later, I went to another friend's house and helped her with some paperwork she needed done. I would have rather stayed home, but she needed my help before her meeting that night, so I went. The time was rather short, and she doesn't really gossip, so that also went well. She got a little frustrated with something she received in the mail, and with a sense of humor we moved right past it. She, herself, is a blessing in my life.

The weather was very cold, but invigorating. I grew up just south of Chicago, so I appreciate some cold weather as I get to wear my heavy coats, sweaters and boots, which I love.

My heater worked in the car, which was iffy a few weeks ago just as it started to get cold.

The clouds and sunset were amazing. I stayed in one lane while driving and had a peaceful trip. I spent the leisurely drive thinking of all the things and people in my life I have to be thankful for and the absolute abundance I have been blessed with. Okay, that does not automatically pay my bills, but I appreciate every ounce of abundance I do have in my life...which is a lot by any standards.

Each day brings us new opportunity to react to the minute by minute happenings. Each day gives us the opportunity to react better than the last time, or better than we usually would. Every single day brings us the chance to look for and find the magic and miracles we *are* given, and to be thankful for each and every one of them. OR...we can just go through the day as usual, self-absorbed with what we have to do, what we have to do for others, or what we should be doing. Each day we make those choices.

Every time you awaken you have the choice as to what kind of a day you will have, how you will spend it, and how you will affect all those who cross your path. If you want this new chapter of your life to be different, more meaningful and more productive, then you need to remain aware in each passing moment of the day...and make your choices accordingly. Soon you will join me in *knowing* what a great difference a day can make.

8. Sense of humor—keep it handy. My entire life, my mom told me that you can get through anything in life if you keep your sense of humor, and I have always found that to be true even though many things in life are not funny. There is no humor in divorce, death, poverty, loss of job, or severe illness.

When my oldest son TJ died at age twenty-two, it was

unexpected, traumatic, tragic and overwhelming. I spent the first three days on so much Valium that they are fuzzy. After that, the grief seemed unbearable, but as with anything, life goes on. My parents stayed with Jim and me, and while they respected the enormity of what had happened (and were also grieving), they made me focus on the good times with TJ, and some of the silly things he had said or done...or the rather stupid things he thought were a good idea at the time. I still cried, but with laughter in my heart. T.J. was such a blessing to our lives, and that has been my focus these past ten years since his death. Just writing about him brings me to tears, but now I am able to switch quickly to the good times, his smile and his wit. It doesn't take the pain away, and it doesn't make me miss him in my life any less, but it makes it bearable to think of something funny he *always* did or said, thinking he was *so cool*.

In 1969 at age forty-four, my Mom had breast cancer and a radical mastectomy (she is soon to be eighty-two years old...by the grace of God). That whole cancer thing is so scary and traumatic to everyone, but we got through it, and life went on. I remember being at a fair one time not too long after that and there was a booth with balloons and a large sign over it that said, *Bust One and Win!* My Mom (goofball that she is) walked right over to the booth, and we all followed her, wondering why she would go there (not a game player at fairs). She asked in her loudest voice, "I have one bust, what do I win?" The guy just looked at her. We just shook our heads and walked quickly away. That's my mom.

Another time she was in the ocean in Hawaii and her prosthesis (padding in the pocket of her swimsuit on the side of the mastectomy) popped out of her suit, and she started yelling, "My boob, my boob, help...find my boob!" and had everyone in the water, family and strangers alike, looking for her boob. They were all in waist deep water, so Mom went up and sat in the shallow water and sure enough, here it came floating in. She was very thankful for the help and having it back.

Mom always has a sense of humor. It's one of her many gifts that she has always shared with our family and anyone she met, and now she is sharing it with you, through me.

Life goes on, no matter what trials or tribulations occur. You need to deal with it, then sit back and review it briefly, looking for the humor that *will* be there somewhere, and focus on that. It doesn't change anything, but it sure puts you in a better, more positive and receptive (for God's blessings and abundance) place. It does not help anything or anyone to indefinitely be upset, depressed, grieving, angry, frustrated or at a loss of what to do. Wayne Dyer, in several of his books, tells us, "Change the way you look at things, and the things you look at will change." He is such a wise man.

Mile Markers - Part Two:

> You know you are climbing out of the valley when…
>
> - You start getting positive response…from some*one*, then some*one* else…
> - People are returning your phone calls more often (you have to realize they have more to do than address your issue). Even if they call to say no, you are getting the lines of communication open and some of the no's out of the way. This is progress.
> - People are willing to refer you to someone else that might be (more?) interested in your plan, and/or more appropriate
> - Your enthusiasm returns, which makes all the difference in the world. People respond to your enthusiasm for whatever you are trying to do in life. Usually, they will help you if they can, or at least remember to tell someone about you when it is appropriate. Enthusiasm equals free publicity in my opinion.

- You finally start connecting with the people who can assist to make your plan a success (usually from your enthusiasm and focus, referrals, or new ideas you thought of during the down time in the valley)
- You are confident that others will benefit from your idea or plan and you can convey that to others easily
- Even if others are not involved, they obviously admire your enthusiasm and determination to succeed in sharing your gift(s).
- You are grateful for each day, and the magic and miracles (large or small) contained therein. You get up earlier and can't wait to get started.
- Your main focus is on helping others, so everyone you talk to or meet during your day is of great interest to you. You automatically share your joy of life and peacefulness through your interaction with them. You are a benefit to their day whether you realize it or not.
- You remember to "Let go, and let God" and know, with everything in you, that one way or another things will work out. That doesn't mean sit on the couch eating Cheetos; you have to put in the effort to be productive. It does mean by just taking one step at a time, *knowing* you are not alone, you will reach your goal. Not necessarily on your schedule, but you *will* get there how and when you are suppose to. Patience is the most difficult ingredient to any success.

One phone call is all it took to turn a struggling recruiting business into a great success. When I had a recruiting business, I kept making calls and making calls, and one day I got the answer I was looking for in requests for contractors and it was all uphill from there. Having the patience and stick-to-it-tiveness to keep on keeping on, when there seems like the results will probably be the same, will eventually get you where you are going. If you are focused on the good of others in your goal, you will go higher and farther than you even imagined.

Being productive does not necessarily mean physically doing something. It can also mean learning something, self improvement, stretching, growing, planning, or testing. You may have the best idea in the world, but no clue how to get it out to others so you will need to research what that will entail. Research marketing techniques, or find someone who will partner with you, brainstorm with you, teach or show you how to make it happen. You may be the best business person in the world, or a marketing guru, but your idea is something you will need to practice and improve upon before sharing it with others. You can research what others have done to implement something similar. Maybe finding financing is the issue you need to address. Find your possible resources.

There is always something new and exciting to learn, but if you feel that you already have the knowledge you need, then by all means just proceed. You will, I guarantee you, find that there is something else you need to learn before you see success. Most likely it will be in the self improvement area, a fascinating subject we all need interest in on a regular basis. It's something I have needed work on most of my life. We all do.

Throughout my childhood, all through grade school and high school, I cannot remember one time I ever thought about, dreamed of or wondered about "what I would be when I grew up?" I guess I just lived life as it came and enjoyed it day by day, week by week. I must have subconsciously assumed that I would just be me. A belief I still have, and I still follow (much to the chagrin of most who know me), wherever it takes me. I do know there are a plan and a purpose to my life. Where I have been, with all the trials, tribulations, and triumphs are part of that plan. As I said in the introduction, I have experienced the highest of high and among the lowest of low in my life. And yet, here I sit on my couch, writing about happy, productive ways to share our gifts with others. God does work in mysterious ways, and it is always a joy to me to see what's next.

All of a sudden I was a senior in high school (like I didn't know that was going to happen?) and everyone was asking me what I was going to do next? I had NO plan, one way or the other. College hadn't crossed my mind, so I had not applied when everyone else did. My grandfather, Pa, had been in and out of hospitals many times in his life and he greatly admired nurses. I loved him to death, and I thought "I could be a nurse...that would make Pa proud." I applied to nursing school, but only cared if I got in or not because it would give me an answer to what I would do next. Wonders of wonders, they accepted me and I became a nurse. Good answer, as I absolutely loved being a nurse, and helping others.

I stayed in nursing until TJ was born, then became a stay at home mom. Raising TJ and Jason was a much better job. Having been out of nursing for so long, during and after my divorce I did many other things, from Mary Kay Cosmetics to waitressing, and finally back to nursing. I eventually went into management in medical related companies, which included sales. From there, I exercised my entrepreneurial gifts and have worked both unbelievably successfully, and unsuccessfully, on my own ever since. I have taken jobs here and there when someone else talked me into it, but most of the time has been spent working on my latest idea, which makes my son Jason CRAZY. He is planning what he will do with me in my old age, since he thinks I have no plan of my own. Well, I don't right now, but it will come to me when I need it.

If you sit quietly and think about the path you have taken it all makes sense to where you are today. After my divorce, I moved from south of Chicago, where I had grown up, to central Illinois where my parents had relocated. That required return trips to Chicago, on one of which I met my husband Jim. I had been single for seven years and didn't date much, but he was a charmer and we got married seven months to the day after we went out for the first time…all by the Grace of God. We lived in central Illinois for several years until I got a job offer in St. Louis, Missouri.

We relocated for my new job, and it was through my job in that office building that I met my friend (later to be partner) Joe while we were boating on the Mississippi river. Joe had a VERY successful recruiting business. He recruited information technology people for large and small companies. He kept telling me that I should do what he does. Two years after we came to St. Louis, I hated my current job and called Joe to ask what it was he did exactly? He explained, and I thought, *If he can do it, I can do it,* and I talked it over with Jim and took the leap. Joe and I started another IT recruiting company. With his money and my effort, it became a success. I bought him out later, and he retired.

I had no clue when Joe and I started the business what I was doing, but I am a fast learner, good with people, and determined as they come. Jim was totally supportive, even though it took me a year to get the new business Joe and I started up and running well. But it was all uphill from there! I took a startup company from zero to over a five million dollar company in eighteen months…by the Grace of God. It was a lot of hard work, but also a lot of fun. During this time, Jim started a company called *Laderak* in our garage (ladder racks for those men and women running around with a ladder hanging out of the back of their pickup truck).

The year after we "hit it big" (HUGE) financially with the recruiting company, TJ, died. Immediately after that Jim's health, which was poor to begin with, got drastically worse and we were in and out of hospitals and dialysis centers for the next two years. He died exactly two years after TJ. Then the whole thing (both deaths) hit me and I was not "with the program" for quite some time. While I went to work every day, I certainly was not functioning properly; but everything happens for a reason. It's a substantial shock to your system to realize that no matter how much money you make or have, no matter what you own or even are able to do for others, it doesn't stop death and tragedy from being part of your life. "Life was good," but it didn't matter.

For many reasons, I closed the recruiting business, sold the house and decided I would now do *Lakeraks*. Moving forward took way longer than I anticipated. Lack of enough money to proceed put an end to that. I read the *One Minute Millionaire* while trying to figure how to make things work out better, and I immediately sat down and wrote *Pulling It Together*, which I felt took books like *OMM* and put the information in everyday terms, telling you the reality of it, not just the hype. Lack of enough money by that time, even for postage let alone publishing, put an end to that.

I was at Rotary one day, and wondered how a deaf member knew what the speaker was saying? The president, sitting next to me, said that he read lips. The speaker wasn't moving his lips much, so I know he wasn't getting the message. By four o'clock the next morning I had outlined an entire communication system for the deaf that would allow children or adults to be able to participate in any class, meeting or function...again by the Grace of God, I might add. I am definitely not that smart. Lack of money to even get the patent put a temporary end to that. I will, somehow, someway make this a reality some day as it can and will help so many people live a fuller life...by the Grace of God.

Three women friends and I were going to a St. Louis Rams football game one weekend and none of us could find anything we liked to wear. I sat in my friend's garage one morning and thought about starting a woman's sportswear company that would cater to women other than sizes 2-6 (all you could find in the stores). I had grown up around the business, with my Dad in clothing sales, and knew enough to get it started. I talked to an acquaintance, Judy, now a treasured friend, and she agreed that we would do it together. Even though she invested to get us started, in the end it was a lack of money to continue that put at least a temporary end to that.

So many ideas, with so much talent to get them started. Lack of adequate funding is *always* a show stopper. I keep saying that everything happens for a reason, and I believe that. So there has to be a reason when everything else seems right that things go wrong. Maybe your idea doesn't take a lot of financing (many don't), and you can't move forward. Perhaps you have all the financing in the world, but it still doesn't work out as you planned. No matter what the block is, there is something you have not learned to be able to attract the success you are looking for. I am an expert in getting almost there on a project, so please believe me when I say again that the block most likely will be in the self awareness area, a fascinating subject we all need interest in on a regular basis. I know that now, I didn't know that then.

I have been in the valley so long, so many times, and have been totally confused as to why things would not move forward for me financially, and decided that I had to find an answer. There was obviously something that I was missing. I had been given great ideas, found others to work with me on them, but nothing worked out right. So I would move on to something else. This has gone on for the past five years.

One thing I know from so many years in sales is that if you need money, sales is the hardest business to be in…there is no way to mask the desperation you feel to get the sale when you need the sale. You can smile, be gregarious as possible, know your product inside and out and have the most convincing sales pitch, but there is always an underlying sense of need. Your constant follow-up is their first clue. You'd like it to come off as your being thorough, but they know by the third call they have not returned what the deal is. What is the answer to this dilemma?

Stop trying so hard and go within. Everything you need to move anything forward is there…in you. The answers are not in anyone else, but in your own level of faith and trust. I have learned that the hard way. Don't reinvent the wheel...read (or listen to on tape) all the motivational or spiritual books you can find by any author that you identify with.

You can try this and try that, but until you realize that it is the Spirit (of God) with in you that is the answer you are looking for, things will probably remain blocked. Some people feel that these answers are located only in the Bible. Some people feel that "religions" are just too structured (just man-made rules), and their personal relationship with God is just as powerful, but more spiritually oriented.

I believe that God accepts worship from each of us in our own way. He doesn't criticize, judge, or turn away anyone who believes in Him, no matter how they practice their faith. I do not believe he has check-in lines, like in Wal-Mart, with those who believe this over there...those who believe that line two, etc. He loves us all, and He welcomes us all. He is with each of us here on earth, and will always be with each of us. When we pursue this knowledge, within ourselves, of the expectations of living in spirit with God, we learn to live differently. We see what it takes to succeed at anything in life, and realize that there isn't anything you can't accomplish.

Okay, you are ready to go...you have learned what you needed to in the valley and are all packed (with knowledge) for the next leg of your journey. Most people would probably choose a foothill or two to try initially, but then there are those who will go straight for one of the highest mountains. You are excited, but don't forget that climbing out of the valley has its own set of rules:

- Never step on or over someone on your way up
- Look for magic and expect to find miracles along every step of the way. They will be there, and they will be your foot holds as you climb.
- Appreciate everyone and everything that aids in your climb

- Be thankful daily for your progress and blessings
- Help anyone you meet on your climb if they need it…what you give out always comes back tenfold
- Remain humble, you aren't doing this alone
- Give others credit whenever you can, there is always enough to go around
- Share your joy and excitement with everyone you meet. Your enthusiasm may trigger just what they need to move forward on their journey

Living "By the Skin of Your Teeth"

The neatest thing about getting it together is no longer living "by the skin of your teeth." I have done that so many times in my adult life that I wore them plum out and now have a full set of dentures. If you ever see me in person, please admire my smile, and it will have been worth it.

You can tell you are no longer living by the skin of your teeth when (again, not a redneck joke, although it may sound like one for those of you who have never been there)…

- The phone actually works, and the internet!
- There is really more than one roll of toilet paper in the house (a whole package, even)
- You don't have to feel sheer panic when the garage door opener doesn't work the first time (you know the electricity bill *is* paid, and the lights *will* come on)
- Your heart doesn't stop every time the door bell rings (there is no one with horrible news or a major hassle for you on the other side)
- You don't feel like throwing up every time a car door slams outside your house
- The TV always works (without those "pay your bill

before we shut this off" messages popping up all the time)
- The water keeps flowing throughout the house (and the toilets *will* flush just fine)
- You have cereal and milk at the same time (what a treat)
- There is a choice of fresh and just bought food in the house for meals (instead of a weird combination of whatever you bought once)
- You can pay and file your bills (instead of making piles and shuffling them around until the pile is so big you just shove it in a bag and out of sight)
- When you get a positive response in business, you actually have a working vehicle, with insurance even, and the gas to get there (major improvement)
- You are not in a flat panic about eviction each and every month
- Your kids do not have to choose between eating this week or replacing shoes with holes and outgrown clothes
- There is laundry soap
- There is an extra can of coffee and lots of Coffeemate Lite
- You can actually get the mail knowing that there will not be shut off notices or other bad news

The list goes on and on. To some of you it seems like a joke, but it's not. I can hear others say, "Yep. Been there, done that," as too many people have. And that is only a very small portion of the problems and issues that can and do arise when you are living "by the skin of your teeth."

Many of you wonder who would actually live like that…and why? Many people think that living like that is a personal choice and those people are just lazy. I guess there are situations like that, but I can assure you that they are not reading this book, or any other. They are not concerned about their situation and are not interested in changing it.

These "wise" people think that if you just get two jobs, or three, then all of the problems would be solved. But would they work two or three jobs if the need arose? They would probably not because if the need suddenly arose, they would be in the same frame of mind as those who are there now. Mystified and amazed, wondering how do I change this?

When your back is against the wall and your needs are great, life takes on a whole different slant. No matter how much you pray, read, or you learn that it's in your beliefs, thoughts and attitude that you attract things to you; sometimes you just can not stay above the feeling of doom which just brings more scarcity your way. You can't seem to find a job that will catch you up *and* pay your bills, which seems an insurmountable task...not to mention how rare those jobs usually are to begin with.

If one positive thing happens in a day, life is good and you feel like it is a big light at the end of the tunnel. This may or may not be true, but you feel like there is hope. On those days when nothing but more pressure seems to arrive, you wonder if and how you are going to make it? You try to get above it, and many times you are able to, but it's so hard. Some of you can't begin to imagine that feeling, but many of you can.

In today's world, there are so many people under pressure they never had before. With mergers, consolidations, or just the rising cost of everything, many people are in a totally different boat than they used to be. Can you tell who these people are in your day? Do you really care? Unless it is a family member or very close friend, you probably will have no clue unless you pay attention to what people are really saying.

No one at Rotary, Chamber meetings or church would have any idea if I was in trouble or not. I arrive smiling, make pleasant conversation and leave. That's how it goes. Someone you see on a regular basis could really be in financial difficulty, emotional distress or severe physical pain and most of the time you would not know. How sad is that? People you see on a regular basis do have needs, whether they express them or not. They may be issues with family, kids, money, work, or their life in general, but we all have issues to deal with. No one's life, no matter how it appears on the surface, is free of any issues at all. Many people in this day and age, in actuality, are one paycheck away from total financial disaster.

It is said that "the need for money is the root of all evil." That evil is in the form of worry, doubt and fear of the future which many times causes ill health, arguing, and bad behavior in all family members. It causes the inability to focus at work, depression, and hopelessness. It's hard to emotionally "get above" any one of those things, let alone several or all of them, without the love and support of others. Just knowing they love you and care is a boost.

Some people inherit money or a business, marry well, win the lottery, or have worked themselves silly and have become successful. Some of them remember when things were not so great financially, but many never give having less a thought unless or until their circumstances change. Illnesses and death happen, and children or other family members or close friends have difficulties that need to be dealt with, no matter what your financial situation is at present. Having money does not guarantee anything, except your ability to spend it.

I am not saying that you should take on everyone else's issues; after all, they do not really belong in your box. Awareness of what people are really saying to you, caring about all others, listening if someone needs to talk, and showing love and support to another is all it takes to make an enormous difference in someone's life. Just a few minutes of your time, you are not adopting them. None of us are so busy we don't have a few minutes to encourage another person. If you are, you may want to rethink your priorities.

You do not necessarily have *to do* anything. The fact that you care, and may be willing to brainstorm and talk through options (without determining what direction *you* think *they* should take) is encouraging. Listen to others with the intention of truly hearing what they mean, not just what they are saying. Chose one other person to get to know better and find out about their life. Imagine what a difference it would make if we all did this. Most people have the tendency to pass kindness shown to them on to another. What a great chain reaction to start!

As with so many things in life, there may be no telltale signs. These people come from all backgrounds; all shapes, sizes or color. They may "seem a little down," but they are not just having a bad moment. Most of the time, they will put their issues away when you are talking to them. When there is just something that keeps nudging you to look closer, it may be that your willingness to pay closer attention to others is paying off.

The ability to care is another gift we are given in abundance. If you offer to grab a cup of coffee or something, and they refuse, don't take it personally...you gave your gift and they received it (and appreciated it). They now know they can call you, and you have added to their available support system, which means the world to them. Don't be surprised if you get a call just to run some ideas by you. You have made them feel safe enough to seek out your opinion, and they just may.

If this has never happened to you, you may be wondering why these people don't just come out and tell others what is going on with them. How you would feel if it were you, and your circumstances changed drastically? You would not be willing to share that with the world, but you would grab any sincere lifeline offered. The difference between someone just wanting to be in the know about what is going on (just being nosey) and honest caring is so obvious to those who need help. If your inquiry is not from the heart, don't make it...just move on. You will find someone else, someday, that you know you are to help, and you will.

If you have ever been in that situation, find another that is still there to help. You recognize the signals. Whenever I had money to function, the first thing I did was call Sheila, Heather, and Kathy and make sure they were okay. I couldn't pay their bills, too, but when you have literally not a dime, $5, $10 or $20 is a miracle. $50-100 is like you won the lottery. They returned the favor all the time…it's what friends do for friends, and the saying was always, "Because I have it and you don't." As each of us climbs our mountain things have changed, but none of us will ever forget the lean times, or take our blessings and abundance for granted!

If you are still there, hang on. Have faith, and trust in God like you never have before. Help others, and be thankful for the abundance you do have in your life. Everywhere you look you will see the magic and miracles you have been given and they will grow and grow.

You, too, will be climbing your next mountain and finding your right path before you know it.

Everyone should remember that a small kindness may mean the world to another. If someone's answers are always vague, that is your first clue that in one way or another they may be barely hanging on. The cause could be any number of reasons, but chances are they are desperate inside about something and they just may be living moment by moment, and day by day, "by the skin of their teeth."

...and Friends

When I talk about friends, I most assuredly include my family. My family members are also among my *best* friends, even when some of us don't get to talk or see each other often. Good or bad, they are always there in a real pinch, or to share successes with. In that, I am so very blessed, as it is not the case for everyone.

When the day comes that you realize there is a difference between where you are in life, and where you want to be, your first line of support is your friends (and hopefully family). You don't have to be living by the skin of anything for this day to come. It could be something you read or something you heard someone say, it could be a change in someone you know, or see on a regular basis, that inspires you to evaluate your life. It could be one or more of any number of things, and the evaluation could be gradual. When that day comes, you generally will feel confused and in need of support for the immediate future. Real change is scary to anyone. Choose carefully who you turn to.

When your life appears to be going well, there are many more "friends" to choose from. When things aren't so great, money gets tight, issues arise that you are upset or worried about, or your interests change, it is amazing how that number dwindles all of a sudden.

I have found that friends are comfortable if you act like you always have, and do what you always do. When you change your habits and patterns, or focus, you make them nervous and they are less interested in being part of your world.

When you decide to make changes in your life (spiritual changes will always lead to literal changes), some of your friends and family will support you, and some will not. Some will tell you what you should be doing and walk away if you don't follow their advice. Let them walk away. If they are meant to be in your life, they *will* return.

Everyone is on their own journey, whether they acknowledge that or not. You will find yourself gravitating to those who are in the same neighborhood as you intend to be, and away from those who need to remain where they are. Since we attract each and every person or thing into our life, those friends who leave were there for a reason, but now that reason is no longer valid and they will be gone. It is said that everyone is in our life for a reason, some just for a season, and some for life. Very few will probably be around for life, but that is as it should be. Remember, there are no mistakes.

For those of you who have never been truly WEALTHY (financially), let me assure you that it has its ups (you can always pay bills, and can pretty much do and buy what you want), but it also has its downs. You never really know if all these "friends" are hanging around because of the money, or to be with you. You always feel awkward because the people you like to do things with can never afford to do what you can, and want, to do. You almost always pick up the tab (its nothing for you to do that), but that in itself is awkward. This list also goes on and on. I'm sure some of you are thinking, "Poor babies. Give me those problems and I wouldn't care," and some of you are saying, "Yep. Been there, done that."

It's been amazing to me to think back on the people formerly in my life and ponder when they arrived, how it went while they were there, and when/why they left? If you take a break and do this, quietly, alone, you will have many more than one "Ahhaaa!" moments.

Their arrival in your life, and whether they stay or depart, is all based on your needs at the time. Sometimes you control it, sometimes you don't. That's just life.

I believe that we attract others into our lives that are a mirror image of ourselves in some way or another. If you focus on it, I am sure you will agree, even though it is not the most comfortable subject to contemplate.

YEARS ago, when I was a Mary Kay consultant, I joined in April, and although I loved it and was doing rather well, I stopped focusing in September of the same year due to my divorce. When I went to convention in Dallas that January, I didn't even respond, until someone poked me when they announced that I was number one in recruiting and number two in sales for the unit. Imagine my surprise! Our unit was ranked number seventeen in the entire company, so I had done well. Be that as it may, I was still not a director. You see, I recruited women like myself who were either going through a divorce, or had just gotten one. We supported each other because we understood. They required you to recruit six *qualified* consultants to be a director at that time. When I had five qualified, they changed it to nine. When I had eight qualified, they changed it to twelve and when I had eleven, they changed it to fifteen. Needless to say, I was DONE. It was not that I couldn't sell, recruit, train and lead the women, but I recruited all women with constant problems, both personally and financially...just like me at the time.

After my divorce, I moved and hung out with nurses and hospital staff, because I was a nurse at the time.

Jim was right where I was when we met. We both had decent jobs, had been single for years, waiting for that right person to come along. We had a great time building our lives together and supporting each other through thick and thin; and there were LOTS of both in our thirteen years together.

After Jim died, I stayed within my close circle of personal friends for a long time, but finally made myself move on. In my new apartment and new life, I made myself go out and meet new people. I joined Chambers of Commerce and got involved, and the Rotary with meetings every week. I met very nice people and enjoyed those activities, but the new friends I hung out with were all single women I had met.

My name is Betty, but Jim called me Betsy and introduced me as Betsy to all. It just evolved, so all my new friends now call me Betsy. In that apartment, I met another "Betsy" (divorced). I made a new great friend, Ann (separated then, now divorced), at a little bar I found and liked to socialize in (I am not a big drinker, but the people were nice and it was a comfortable place to have fun). Add to the mix my little angel, Sheila (divorced), who I met at Chamber, and you have our little group for the summer. We all went everywhere together and some called us "the rack pack." If any one of us would arrive alone first, we would immediately be asked where the rest were...that kind of thing. If Sheila and Ann arrived first, the question then became, "Where's the Betsys?" We spent a large portion of the summer at the pool together, and just ran and chased. It was a fun summer.

Betsy and I still see each other on a fairly regular basis. She now has a man in her life, but we so enjoy each other's company, we make the time to spend together when we can. I still see Ann now and then, and she is also still a great friend. We just have such different priorities right now that we aren't together a lot. Sheila and I talk every day and see each other all the time. We are both still single and in the same neighborhood, each with our own intentions. It just makes sense to support and help each other as best we can, and we do. I love them all, and I am so blessed to have them, each in their own way, in my life.

Betsy, Ann and Sheila never see or talk to each other, and probably wouldn't unless I brought them together again, or they bumped into one another. While I have a special relationship with each of them, they do not have things in common with each other. That's how it works, it seems. But it was a fun summer, and one I will remember forever.

I was very fortunate to be able to work with Wings of Hope for a few months last year, scheduling the flights for their Medical Air Transport Service. What a great group of people. The staff is small, the number of regular volunteers is large, and they all pull together for the benefit of those less fortunate in the Midwest and around the world. What a cool job is that? I was unable to remain there, financially, as they are a Not for Profit organization, and I am not...bills to pay and all that. I will remain as active as I can at any given time and continue to count them all as a blessing in my life. I know I was led there, and blessed with that position, to meet another group of wonderful friends that were in tune with my need to help others. (You can check them out at www.wings-of-hope.org)

While at Wings, I met Lillian (also a widow for many years). Lillian and I go out to eat usually at least once a week and attend different functions together. She is from the area, so she has developed interests in a wide variety of things and is aware of places to go that would never cross my mind. She and I have a lot in common, but the neatest thing is being able to explore her world with her, which fills my need for new things and adventure. What a blessing she is to my life.

While in Florida one winter, I met Bernie Rhodes, author of *"D.B. Cooper, the Real McCoy."* It was by absolute fate that we were both in the same place at the same time. He and I are still great friends. How fortuitous to have a published author to cheer me on with my intention of writing. It is his presence in my life that is partly responsible for my steely determination to see this through, sooner rather than later; he is a blessing for sure.

Grace is my accountant and has been one of my best friends for fifteen years. She is there in the good times, to keep me straight financially, and the bad times as well. She was one of the first to arrive after TJ died, was there for me when Jim died, and we will always be there for each other no matter what. Friends come and go, but Grace is a keeper. She is a special gift to me from God.

Obviously, many, many other people have come and gone over the years. We had something in common that attracted us to each other at the time, but lives, interest, focus and goals all change. Some people you still remain friends with, some you don't. Some just fade away, and that is the end of it. If you always remember that everything does (or does not) happen for a reason, and that there are no mistakes in these things, it makes the ebb and flow of people in your life make sense. If you wonder why this person is or that person was in your life, look harder and you will see a reflection of yourself in some way.

This can be a good thing or bad, because if you are angry or judgmental all the time, those are the type of people you will attract and hang out with. That is probably why people who are church oriented like to participate in church activities, as the people they are then involved with are on the same page. If you are interested in art, you will gravitate towards people, places, and things that involve art, or the appreciation of art. It just works that way. Again you have a choice whether to continue as you always have or to honestly evaluate your interests at this time in your life and focus on those for this new chapter of your life. If your current friends do not share those interests, it's okay...you *will* make new friends.

True friends are the ones who hang around through good and bad; through thick and thin, and the changes you make in your life. They are supportive and loving; they are kind and help you find your sense of humor when you need to. They are helpful and are willing to share what they have with you, without a moment's hesitation. They give hugs when you need them most. Their love for you is unconditional.

You have set new goals, and as you see success arriving you need to remember a song (I think learned in Brownies, as it seems like I've known it all my life) which goes, "Make new friends, but keep the old. One is silver and the other gold." If there is any more to it, I don't remember that part, but the message is one to always keep in mind. You won't have to wonder which "old" friends you are supposed to keep. They will just still be there...always, even if there are great lengths of time between contacts.

As friendships change, so do relationships. First we are children, then adults—many with children of our own, and before we know it we are taking care of our elders, then we are the elders!

Being a child and having a child are such different perspectives on life. When I was a kid we wouldn't think of calling any adult by their first name. Our parent's good friends were always "Aunt Betty" and "Uncle Ed." Manners were a must, and being sassy was one thing, but you were never outright rude or disrespectful to your parents or any adult. You just didn't do it. Not to say that we were angels by any stretch of the imagination, but there were things you did and things you just did not do. If your parents said no, that was the end of that; well, after a little whining and still not getting your way. But then it was over.

I think when you pass on those values to your children, they grow up and say, "I'll never do that with my kids," and I do believe they, as well as their children, end up paying the price. I know there were a lot of times when the boys were very young that I let things slide just because my parents wouldn't have. But I figured out pretty quickly that it doesn't work that way. They needed the structure and rules of life, the discipline along with the love, and to learn that they would not get to do what they wanted if they mouthed off or acted disrespectfully. That was the kiss of death for them in my book. All kids need boundaries. Once you set the boundaries and stick to them no matter what, it doesn't take long for kids to figure out what is okay, and what is not going to be tolerated.

When I was a single mom with two small boys, I would say no and then have to listen to them go on and on why I should have said yes instead. It drove me crazy, and sometimes it was just easier to give in and change my mind. When I realized how destructive that was to all of us, I learned to tell them that I would think about it, listen to all their reasons why they wanted to do something, then make my decision…and then I could stick to it, no matter what. They quickly learned that if the answer was no, it really meant NO.

As I observe kids today, many are as nice and pleasant as could possibly be…as long as they are getting their own way. Boy and girls of all different ages. You always hear the parents say, "He is such a good boy," or "She is such a delight." Well, yes, when they can do anything they want, eat only what they want, go where they want when they want, what's not to be nice about? But, as soon as the parent says no, this other kid emerges who is rude, nasty, defiant and mean. They act like that because they can. They have learned that they do not have to do what is asked of them, and if they act badly enough they will still be able to go where they want and do what they want because it is easier to let them do it than teach them bad behavior is not okay, and stick to your guns. What are parents thinking?

When a child learns that he or she does not really have to do chores, keep their room clean, do homework, eat what is for dinner, or behave properly and they still get to participate in all the activities they want to, the parent has definitely lost control. The saddest thing about that is what kind of an adult is this child going to be when they do not respect anyone or anything, not even themselves? Parents need to give their children the gift of boundaries and discipline. Its nerve racking at times, but it's free and we have it in that gift to give in abundance. Everyone benefits, and God would smile.

Having grown children who are married with children, is another change to the relationship.

You are no longer in charge, and they will do what they have decided is right. As a grandparent, when things happen that you would have done differently, you need to remember what a good friend told me right after TJ was born. She said, "Honey, they grow up in spite of you, not because of you." So it is with all generations to follow.

Enjoy the good times, love them to death and let it go. It's not your responsibility, in most cases. Make the rules for your house, and that's what happens when anyone is there...kids and grandkids or visitors. Whether they come and go, or are staying or living with you, it's your rules they have to abide by. That doesn't mean you can't spoil them sometimes, it just means that letting them do as they please does not help them learn and grow into responsible adults. Kids know where and when they can and cannot act badly. If God has given us the gift of children and grandchildren, then we are expected to do what is right, not what is easy, to guide them with all the love we have been given to share. Loving them does not mean letting them do whatever they want, it means loving them enough to teach them life's rules, respect, and God's love for them.

The elderly who now need help are as vulnerable as the little ones. It is so hard for them to transition into one who needs from the one in charge and caregiver. Many Senior Citizens do not have family left or that live near to them. If you don't have an elderly family member in need of assistance from you, or you live too far away from them, you can always find someone to help out. Nursing homes are full of people who have no one to care about them. Hospitals and neighborhoods are also full of people with no visitors, and no one that seems to care. A couple hours a week of your time spent with someone who has needs but no one to fill them is definitely sharing the gift of your time and the abundance of love God gave you to share. If we each adopted one extra person to spend even just an hour a week with, no one would ever be left alone in life. God would smile...again.

Many of you are single, and have collected an assortment of "just friends" of the opposite sex. Personally, my "just friends" section is full to overflowing. You meet someone, and maybe date a few times or for a while, and decide this is not going to be permanent and agree to just be friends. There's an enormous amount of transition just in that one relationship. You go from the excitement of meeting, to the anticipation of that first date, to getting to know more about each other, spending time together, and deciding that you are in different places in your life. No one's fault, just not meant to be, and life goes on. Some "just friends" remain in your life and some just fade away. As your interests and goals in life change, so does your list. Amazing how that works.

Long term relationships also change on a regular basis. When someone is in your life for years, you do love them unconditionally whether you want to or not. They probably have done things that you didn't like, but you love them anyway. They have probably said things you really had a problem with, but there they still are. You can personally grow and change and they will remain, as that is what healthy long term relationships are about.

In some relationships issues of physical or mental abuse, addictions, neglect or total lack of communication arise. These all need to be dealt with on a personal basis, which will take a lot of self examination, and changes only you can make to improve your life. You have been given the ability to evaluate and make those changes, but you will have to have the determination to live life a different way. You have to set new goals and know that if you ask God to help you achieve them, He will help you and guide you to a new life. It won't be overnight, but it can and will be done...by the Grace of God.

In business, it's imperative to make friends wherever you go. Even if you have a job that does not require networking, you would probably be amazed how many times you can come up with the "who to call for this?" answer for a friend or relative.

Someone you met or someone knows someone...In an interview recently, I was asked how I knew the lady that recommended me to be interviewed. Well, she was a friend of a friend. Sheila and another great friend of mine, Gary, are networkers extraordinaire. You would think they invented it, and they always know someone who knows someone with a possible answer for anything. Some people just enjoy networking, and some just figure schmooze or you lose.

Whenever anything came up that I wasn't totally confident I knew the answer to, I would always call for a consult. I would sit and think through everyone I know to decide who to call. Whether it was family for their opinion, friends for their opinion or who I should call, I could always think of someone to help me decide what I should do next.

Now, however, since learning that the answers are within me, I don't do that anymore. I now know that if I ask, it is given. I just have to be willing to allow success and be receptive to all the magic and miracles that are mine for the asking. Sound like hocus pocus? Many people feel it does. But if you read (or listen) and learn, understand, believe, and choose to live in spirit, you don't just think or hope things will happen...you *know* they will. That *knowing* tells God that you "get it" and you are willing to depend on Him to be the best friend anyone could ever ask for, which He is.

Be open to new connections and they will come. I have been holed up, working on a database for my current project, making follow-up phone calls, or writing for what seems like a long time. While I get totally engrossed in work, and the hours and days fly by, there comes a point where you just need and want more connection to other people. New people in particular are something you look forward to; fresh ideas, more input and, hopefully, more fun. I am finally learning that you can't do everything alone in business.

Teamwork is the answer to get things accomplished, and I am so thankful that God leads me to people and places that have an impact on the next part of my journey. He is so good at what He does, and if you learn to listen and trust His judgment, you will find yourself in places that will lead you to where you need to be.

The current project I have been working on seems stalled, or is at least taking a lot longer than I though it would to be productive. Consequently, I have to turn to other sources of income to pay the bills. I function as an Executive/ Administrative Assistant for one wonderful lady, who, after a year, has referred me to a friend of hers who also needs some administrative help...just when I needed her to. As I was waiting for a response from that scenario, it crossed my mind that there might be a possibility of writing a column in a local journal, so I put feelers out for that through a friend of a friend. I never thought I would actually be writing a book, possibly be a columnist, and helping two adventurous ladies keep their activities organized, but here I am. When I let go of my idea of what life should be and what I should be doing, and became open to all the possibilities there may be, the direction of my life seems to be changing by the day. How exciting and interesting it has become.

What I have been reminded of more than anything in just the past few weeks is to take one day at a time, look for the magic and miracles in it, and appreciate everything and everyone involved in my day. The future will arrive on its own, and will be neater than anything I could have dreamed up. Any "struggles" or issues I am enduring now are for a reason and will benefit me in the end.

The final decisions are yours, but it sure is a lot more fun if you include the people in your life on your journey. Whether they are there for a season, or forever, they are there for a reason. Take advantage of your time with them, whether a lot or a little. Not only do they have a lesson to share with you, you have an opportunity to share your gifts with them.

Recently I met a woman named Gina who is a can-do woman with can-do friends around her. What a gift God gave me when he led me to an event, which I usually would not attend, to meet a new friend who will be an integral part of my life forever.

Back to the Mile Markers - View from the Top

You know you have climbed up high when...

- You can see results from sharing your gift(s).
- The emotional high is constant; it's no longer where you want to be, it's where you are.
- You feel like you can now conquer the world.
- You feel like laughing, smiling and sharing your joy with all.
- You feel the urge to help others attain the same feeling by helping them to attain their goals in what ever way you are able to.
   Resting on your laurels (achievements) does not even cross your mind.
- You can see the horizon and the choice is yours which mountain to climb next.
- The trials and tribulations of the valleys and the climb do not daunt you as to moving forward and higher the next time.
- You are attracting people, places, things and miracles that match the intention of your goals.

- You have no doubt or fear as you have learned faith
and trust in God is the answer.
- You understand that everything does work out for
the best, even if it's not what you had planned.

When you choose your next step, you know issues will arise, and you are confident you will be able to hang in there and get through them. You will know the major pitfalls and avoid them next time. You can look forward to progress from here, without a doubt, that it will happen. In time you will learn to look at anything you want to do and know for a fact that you can make it a reality.

Remember to be aware of others when you are on this high ground. Your time, your knowledge and, sometimes, financial input can make all the difference in the world to someone else trying desperately to climb out of that valley you know so well. When you realize that it can be done, it is your responsibility to encourage others to find within themselves the answers and ability to follow your lead. Never get too busy to offer encouragement to someone else.

NEVER get too big for your britches. For the past year I have gone in places only to be told I needed to call and make an appointment. When I called to make an appointment, the secretary asked what it was about; when I told her, she would most often tell me to send information. I would send information and call back to make an appointment, to be told either that they were not interested (her opinion many times) or the boss was too busy now, call back in six months or whatever. Getting in to see the decision maker is an art in itself.

I used to be the decision maker of a multimillion dollar company, and was never too busy to give someone five minutes to start their pitch. If it was clearly not my responsibility any more (buying office supplies, etc), then I would stop them and walk them to who they needed to talk to. No one on my staff would ever say they were too busy to listen to what someone had to say. If you don't want to spend a lot of time with a "salesperson," then you come out of your office and stand in a general area to hear what they have to say...do not let them come in, sit down and get comfy. There is always a way to honor other's needs and your own. Find that way, and remember that you were not always the one on top.

Now that you are here, you might feel you need a break. Take one, but I guarantee you it will be hard to ever sit and do nothing again. The emotional high of achieving your goals just makes you want to tackle another goal, and then another. You mind never seems to slow down (unless meditating) and the amazement of seeing the mile markers fly by is an absolute joy.

As with anything, the use of your gifts can be expanded upon in some way. Or you may choose to add a different gift and share that. Now that you can see the difference your gifts do make to others, whether they are large or small, you will be excited to repeat the experience. Go for it. what have you got to lose? You certainly have everything to gain.

Until now, I have truly lived by the grace of God, the skin of my teeth...and friends. The grace of God is always there. When we do not fully realize the extent of it, listen to Him talking to us through His spirit within us, or other people He sends with signs or messages, then we end up living by the skin of our teeth, and our friend's help and generosity.

I take big chances, but I expect big results. I probably have more, and lower, valleys and higher hills and mountains to climb because of that. My journey has put me in a position to know, first-hand, the trials and tribulations that come with having no financial reserve. It isn't that I frittered away all the wealth I was given ...I made business decisions that worked for a while, then things changed. My life changed. But looking back on that time, it shows me that my purpose was not what I was doing then. My purpose is in my journey and what I am doing now in writing this book. Helping others is me! Whether it is through this book, the program helping children, then the

Shared Blessing Fund, it is what feels right to me. If one other person is helped by anything I do, I have successfully completed my purpose. Retirement? What's that?

Your goals for this new chapter of your life may be large or small. You may be interested in taking smaller chances at first, until you realize for yourself that there is nothing you can not accomplish. The knowledge that changes need to be made in your life, the desire to make a positive difference, and the ability to do both are God-given gifts. You do have them, and you just need to make the choice to use them.

Of course, we will wrap this up with a list...of things you should never forget:

- The spirit of God is in each of us, and we are all connected by that spirit.
- Treat all others as you would treat God, for He is in them as He is in you.
- Share the unconditional love, forgiveness, and generosity God gives you with others.
- Spread the joy, peace and wisdom of God's love to all others.
- Lead by example, as the world can and will change, one person at a time.
- Know you can do and be anything you can imagine.
- Believe in yourself, your abilities, and in God's presence in your life.
- You attract everything into your life, and it is a mirror of you in some way.
- You are what you think about, and what you put out is what you will get back...good, bad, or indifferent.
- Things happen in God's time, not ours...everything has a season and a reason.
- There are no mistakes.
- God has a better plan for you than you could have ever imagined. Let go, and let God. Be open to a successful conclusion, and let it arrive.

God doesn't discriminate. He loves us right where we are in life. He always has, and He always will. He keeps sending messages to us in different ways. As we are to trust in Him, He trusts in us that one of these times each one of us will "get it," and share it with others.

I love my friends, but I am done having to depend on them, and I am *really done* living by the skin of my teeth. I do now "get it." Today starts a new chapter for me, too…and this one will be strictly by the grace of God. I have learned that He is with me always, and He is also with you. You can find your gifts and share them with others no matter what, or how long it takes. That is our purpose in life. I'm doing it, and you can, too…by the grace of God.

Epilogue

I hate it when you get to the end of a book and there is a two paragraph epilog. It gives you a very brief little idea what happened next. Well, I will share with you in detail what happened next, which will prove that things do work out for the best.

The projects I was working on while writing this book did not work out financially. My wonderful landlord Brian eventually had to tell me that while he really liked me as a person, renting condos was a business for him and he really needed someone who had a real job and could pay the rent *every* month, not catch up once in a while. Bless his heart, I know he hated to have to have that conversation with me...not as much as I hated for him to have to, but everything happens for a reason. I made arrangements on a Wednesday to move and moved the following Saturday. Yes, I completely packed and moved in four days, with the help of my wonderful sister Althea and the financial help of my wonderful mom, Alice. I am a firm believer that work expands to the time available to it, and if I had had six weeks to pack and move, it would have taken me six weeks. I chose four days, and got it done.

I had looked at an apartment in the city (where I have wanted to live all my adult life and had been visualizing for months) and it was still available. I moved into the city on Saturday, a little over a month ago, and have not stopped grinning yet. I LOVE MY NEW PLACE. I walk every day, and when the weather gets nicer, will expand my walking to explore new places. The metro bus stops right across the street and I can take it to events and places all over the city…how cool is that? After more downsizing, which I needed anyway, my furniture fit perfectly. I decorated in a combination of subtle elegance and "apartment funk" and grin every time I walk through the apartment at how neat it all looks. This is a dream come true, which came out of what one would think were a string of horrible events in their life. I told Brian before leaving that maybe things didn't work out for me (they were all great ideas and technically should have worked just fine) because it finally made me bite the bullet and move to the city? I feel so blessed every moment that I am awake and feel like this is where I am meant to be right now, at this time in my life.

Most of my friends think I am crazy for wanting to live in the city, but I do…and my life is about me, not them, so it's okay.

Another thing I have been totally focused on and visualizing with out a single doubt is my receiving the funding for the Shared Blessings Fund. Everything else I have thought of, put together and tried was meant to lead me to the funding I need for that fund. Maybe, just maybe, I am supposed to let go of all the other stuff and believe a little more in what I feel I am to do for others? I have mapped out the fund, and believe with all my heart and soul that this is my purpose for the rest of my life. I am in a perfect position to do that now, and oh, did I mention that there is the perfect (vacant at the moment) facility available for housing the fund in the very next block down the same street I now live on? I walk by it every day, I have peeked in the windows, gone inside and talked to the maintenance man, walked around the grounds and sat on the front steps visualizing working there every day for the benefit of others.

I honestly believe that God (for me), His Universe, whatever you believe in, can and does work things out if you let go and let Him. I trusted that this move was meant to be. I trust that there is now a purpose for me to be here. I believe that, even though there are a couple of offers on the table for that facility, there is still the possibility it will still be available and will house the Shared Blessing Fund that will benefit thousands of people over the years. If not, I will be lead to the right facility which will, in the end, be the right place.

I am researching charities to work with by assisting them in their fund raising efforts. I am listing hospitals and social services organizations that will have the contacts of people who desperately need help financially, due to the reason they need the hospital to begin with. Illness can devastate a family financially, through no fault of their own, and the fund can and will help those in need. I feel like I am one of the most blessed people on earth right now, and even though I can not see the results of my belief at this very moment, I am no less confident that I can and will attract the funding for this project to me. I believe it is on its way, and I am more than ready for it to arrive.

The point is, finding the blessings in everything that happens in your life and focusing on them, not what you don't have or hasn't happened yet. If you just focus on the lack (of anything) in your life, it brings more of that to you, and that is what you will end up with more of. Trust me, I have inadvertently focused on what I lacked for years, and I just kept getting more of the same. I am not living in a fantasy world, I am now just focusing on seeing what can be as what is, and it makes my days better and better. Only good can come from that.

Evaluate your life, find your gifts, dream your dreams, hang out with positive people who encourage you in attaining your new goals, then reach for the moon. It is said by many that if you reach for the moon and miss, at least you are among the stars. The journey you end up on will be amazing and better than you can even imagine.

I am beginning a new journey (at age fifty-seven no less). Soon I can say, "The funding for the Shared Blessings Fund HAS ARRIVED!" I will now focus on getting it set up and open for business, find a location (the one I want or another) and getting some funds to those in dire need. I will try not to be a workaholic this time around, but will do everything in my power to help those who have not yet had all the blessings they are due and deserve. I am so excited to be chosen to lead this effort. I am one of the luckiest ducks in the pond.

If I had my life to live over, I would do it pretty much the same way because now I know that you can always make it when you have the Grace of God on your side, even if it is by the skin of your teeth at times (lessons to be learned, not bad things), and of course, there is always your friends.

About the Author

At fifty-seven, Betty Ferguson is thoroughly enjoying her single life living in the city. She was raised in the Chicago, Illinois area, but has lived in the St. Louis, Missouri area for the past eighteen years. She enjoys reading, exploring, long walks, meeting new friends and, most importantly, finding ways to share her blessings with others.